PRAISE FOR

PASTORING THE FLOCK OF GOD

If you are a pastor beginning your ministry or if you are now preparing for the pastorate, this book needs to be on your must-read list. In this practical handbook, Pastor Jerry Rueb explains how to be an effective pastor by presenting the relevant biblical texts and weaving in the wisdom he has accumulated from decades of pastoral ministry. The result is a trustworthy guide that will help you become a shepherd after God's own heart.

CLINTON E. ARNOLD

Dean and Professor of New Testament, Talbot School of Theology, Biola University, La Mirada, California
Author of *Three Crucial Questions about Spiritual Warfare* and *How We Got the Bible*

Dr. Jerry Rueb is a leader marked by wisdom, passion, and compassion. His heart for the global church is evident within a few minutes of every conversation he and I have. If there is a pastor who cares for pastors in parts of the world where the church is growing, Dr. Rueb is that leader. The growing church worldwide needs mature and healthy leaders for its pulpits, and this book teems with spiritual encouragement and practical advice for this very purpose. For those who understand the need for pastors in the majority world to be nourished and developed as leaders, *Pastoring the Flock of God* is an essential book, a must-read.

BARRY H. COREY

President, Biola University, La Mirada, California
Author of *Love Kindness: Discover the Power of a Forgotten Christian Virtue*

PASTORING THE FLOCK OF GOD

PASTORING THE FLOCK OF GOD

A GUIDE TO
PASTORAL MINISTRY

DR. JERRY RUEB

Published by Jerry Rueb
Long Beach, California, U.S.A.
www.cclb.org
Printed in the U.S.A.

Italics in Scripture quotations are the emphasis of the author.

ISBN-13: 978-1-5323-0720-1

Names and some details have been changed in some of the stories in this book for the sake of privacy.

For additional information please visit www.cclb.org, e-mail pjr@cclb.org, or write to Jerry Rueb at 1000 North Studebaker Road, Long Beach, CA 90815, U.S.A..

16 17 18 19 20 | 5 4 3 2 1

Contents

Foreword

By Habtamu Kedir Umer

African Christianity has been described as a mile wide and an inch deep, a description I do not fully ascribe to. However, one of the most important needs for building up believers in Africa to attain "to the whole measure of the fullness of Christ" (Ephesians 4:13, NIV) is to equip pastors with biblically sound and culturally relevant training, coaching, and mentoring. It is a heartbreaking experience to see a megachurch pastor without appropriate preparation for the ministry. This is a common problem in Ethiopia, other African countries, and beyond.

I had been looking for a model pastor to learn pragmatic and replicable principles from when I met Pastor Jerry Rueb three years ago. In addition to his self-disciplined learning, he has achieved the highest stage on the academic ladder and has more than forty years of experience in pastoral ministries. I have been privileged to experience, observe, and participate in the strategically designed ministries of Cornerstone Church in Long Beach, where Dr. Jerry is the lead pastor.

The desire to write this book was instigated by passionate and consistent dialogues between Pastor Jerry, Cornerstone Church leaders, and leaders of the Ethiopian Kale Heywet Church. This book, *Pastoring the Flock of God*, is intended to holistically equip pastors by providing a broad understanding of pastoral ministry and helping pastors fulfill their God-given mandates. Kale Heywet Church comprises more than eight thousand local churches and eight million members across the country and is the largest evangelical church in Ethiopia. More than 80 percent of its members are children and youth, which emphasizes the urgent need to prepare pastors who are responsible to equip the next generation. The church has a strategic plan to train thousands of pastors, and this book will be used as one of the most important tools in the training process.

One of the common rhetorical questions I have heard about curriculum is related to contextualization—the relevance of Western books in African contexts. Contextualization is an ongoing process that requires active engagement with the constantly changing dynamics of culture and a sound understanding of the Bible. Dr. Jerry was careful to observe cultural contextualization in the preparation of this book. We are in a defining moment in the history of Christianity to design a new paradigm of partnership between Western churches and churches in the global south to fulfill God's mission. It is time to build up our ministry in a partnership that embraces biblical values, including mutuality and reciprocity. The learning philosophy in Pastor Jerry's book is grounded in learning about each other, learning from each other, and learning with each other. Pastor Jerry has developed an intercultural intelligence and a global perspective through his ministry experience in different nations.

This book, *Pastoring the Flock of God*, is a timely answer to the prayers of people who know the season. We are living in a globalized world that is aggressively exclusive to people who believe in absolute truth and Judeo-Christian values. This is also a time for the greatest revival and harvest of souls into the kingdom of God. The resurrected Lord, the ultimate Shepherd of God's flock, instructed Peter to shepherd His sheep. In order to help pastors fulfill their callings, Pastor Jerry has produced a theologically sound, methodologically inspirational, ecclesiologically relevant, and culturally interrelated book. This book is loaded with knowledge, wisdom, strategies, models, and principles that can serve as a blueprint to equip pastors and help them carry out fruitful ministries. I am deeply convinced that this book will be transformative and inspirational for those who dream of bringing sustainable impacts to their lives and ministries.

Preface

When [Jesus] saw the crowds, he had compassion for them, because they were harassed and helpless, like sheep without a shepherd.
MATTHEW 9:36

The church on Earth in the twenty-first century is changing in size and composition with incredible speed. Instant global communication and high-tech devices like computers and smartphones bridge the once-overwhelming gap between the Christian's desire to share the gospel and the unbeliever's search for God on every nation on Earth. Well-designed websites communicate the Christian message with the click of a mouse and offer online discipleship courses in how to become a follower of Christ—all with little or no human interaction or follow-up.

But whether the current progress of the gospel uses traditional methods or embraces the latest technologies, people's hunger for the good news of the gospel is reaching an all-time high. Across the planet followers of Jesus are increasing by more than eighty thousand per day! China now has more followers of Jesus than members of the Communist Party. In Africa the church is growing by thirty-four thousand every day.[1] We are living during the greatest time of harvest ever seen in world history.

With millions of new believers joining the ranks of the church each year, the need for pastors to spiritually feed and tend them is increasing exponentially. Unfortunately, the growth of trained pastoral leaders is not keeping pace with the number of new believers worldwide. Without trained leadership, the impressive harvest could be spoiled and the sheep scattered.

But another harvest spoiler has taken advantage of this present leadership void—and this danger could prove to be the greatest threat facing the church today. The siren voices of personal success are redefining the pastor and his work, creating a conflict with the self-sacrificial example of leadership that Jesus set for us.

For forty years I have been fully engaged, blessed, and honored with the high calling of shepherding congregations in both the United States and Canada. I pastored my first church in Colorado, and later I served in California and then in Vancouver, Canada. In 2001, following the tragic events in New York City on September 11, I felt God's call to start a new church in Long Beach, California, a spiritually resistant area. We began with eight couples, and within ten years the church had become the largest in the city and known for our commitment to world missions and for creatively ministering within our local community.

As I have served in my calling as a pastor, the Lord has led me to other opportunities for ministry. I have been privileged to write several books as well as speak at colleges, conferences, and churches. I am also humbled to minister on the board of Biola University and to serve with other ministries such as the Evangelical Fellowship of Canada Mission Commission, Missions Fest International, Capernwray Bible School, and African Bible Colleges in Uganda. My wife, Sue, a professional educator and author, works alongside me as founder and president of Brain Rehabilitation and Injury Network, a national non-profit organization that provides research, recovery, and residual care to brain-injured adults. In all this ministry, however, one of my greatest privileges is teaching the Word of God honestly and powerfully with the goal of equipping believers to answer God's unique call on each of their lives and to prepare them to declare the gospel to the entire world.

My experience has taught me volumes about the practical side of pastoring. My deeper understanding of the Bible has guided me through troubling times. I've navigated past the subtle cultural, personal, and ecclesiastical wolves who pose a threat to the flock of God, and I've enjoyed the miraculous blessings of phenomenal church growth, community leadership, and worldwide impact, all of which have gone beyond my greatest expectations.

For decades I have also studied the advice of the latest church-growth advocates and read numerous books of "successful" pastors who have presented their model to chart a new course for the church. I've been a witness to trends that appear on the scene as the "answer" to how church is to be done, only to see these fads fade into oblivion. I've observed the proud excesses and the humbling falls of prominent church leaders who have treated the pastorate as an extension of their personal aspirations. I've known fiery preachers who have had the unusual ability to sway a crowd, and I've seen the lives of these pastors outside the pulpit as tragic disasters. Did Jesus say "I will build My church" only to have it dismantled by the people who lead it? There must be a better way! *Pastoring the Flock of God* is designed to address the urgent need for pastors to gain a biblical understanding of God's call to shepherd His flock and humbly embrace the work of leading and caring for God's people.

At a breakfast meeting after the resurrection, Jesus forever placed the highest priority on the work of shepherding. Surprisingly, He did not call Peter to build great buildings or create great institutions. Jesus invited Peter to a movement that would rely on leaders to become God's history-shaping servants. Jesus called intrepid shepherds of God's flock to embrace their primary tasks of nurturing and minding His sheep. At that breakfast on the beach, Jesus challenged Peter, "Feed my lambs. . . . Tend my sheep. . . . Feed my sheep" (John 21:15–17). In that moment Jesus unveiled His single-most important and profound method for sustaining healthy and reproducing Christians: called and qualified pastors who understood and practiced the leadership model of Jesus, the good Shepherd.

What does that model look like? Who fits the qualifications of a shepherd? How is a shepherd to lead? What tools does the shepherd need to lead and feed the sheep? What relationship with the sheep does Jesus expect from His under-shepherds? There has never been a more crucial time since Pentecost in which the church needs to recapture this leadership priority and methodology. The need for godly pastors to shepherd the flock of God has never been more urgent, and the reward for answering the urgent call to be a shepherd has never been more compelling. In 1 Peter 5:1–4 we find from the mouth of Peter, inspired by the Holy Spirit, the promising echo of that early-morning breakfast with the risen Christ:

> I exhort the elders among you, as a fellow elder and a witness of the sufferings of Christ, as well as a partaker in the glory that is

going to be revealed: shepherd the flock of God that is among you, exercising oversight, not under compulsion, but willingly, as God would have you; not for shameful gain, but eagerly; not domineering over those in your charge, but being examples to the flock. And when the chief Shepherd appears, you will receive the unfading crown of glory.

Acknowledgments

Special thanks to Dr. Franklin Graham and the Billy Graham Evangelistic Association for granting permission to translate and print the *Christian Worker's Handbook* for the pastors of the Kale Heywet Church in Ethiopia to use with *Pastoring the Flock of God.*

Deepest thanks to the leadership of the Kale Heywet Church and the nine thousand Ethiopian pastors for whom this book was originally written. May God use *Pastoring the Flock of God* to equip a generation of young and energetic pastors who are poised to lead the fast-emerging church in Ethiopia, Africa, and beyond.

My gratitude to God for my flock at Cornerstone Church in Long Beach, California. Its members have followed me in believing that the Great Commission is worldwide and that God has called us to a greater work than any of us has ever imagined. Their generosity will resonate in heaven forever.

Special recognition to my editor, Becky English, whose exceptional skill and advice challenged me to make the message of this book better, clearer, and more focused. With her tireless professionalism this book was lifted to new heights.

Deepest thanks to my wife, Sue, and my children, Kristin, Jon, and Jana, who have faithfully and fearlessly walked with me through forty years of serving the flock of God. You have shared in the hard work and daunting sacrifices of the pastoral ministry without complaint—and you will surely share in the reward with eternal joy.

1

The Pastoral Leader and the Call to Ministry

Objective: *To define God's call to pastoral leadership, guide prospective pastors to identify God's call, and reveal how the church affirms God's call.*

From the beginning of time, God has called leaders to do His work. It is humbling to consider this fact, since God does not need anyone's help to accomplish His sovereign purposes. Yet He graciously chooses to carefully select special people to accomplish His divine will on Earth. Many of these leaders He calls specifically to pastoral ministry.

In each case, God calls His select leaders personally and often dramatically. For instance, God called Noah to build an ark to rescue his family from coming judgment even before Earth dwellers knew of rain (see Genesis 2:4–6). For His redemptive purposes God called Abram to leave his father's household in Haran and journey to an unknown land of promise (see Genesis 12:1–2). God's call to Abram required him to trust God for the promises of a land, for offspring that would multiply and become a nation, and for the coming blessing of salvation for all nations. Two generations later God used a dream to call Jacob to claim the land upon which he was resting. Jacob called the land Bethel, the "house of God" (Genesis 28:13–17).

These are only three examples of people God called. The entire list of leaders in Scripture reads like a who's who of Bible prophets and apostles, including people like Moses, Gideon, Samson, Samuel, David, Peter, John, Matthew, and Paul.

The big questions for anyone considering pastoral leadership or already serving as a pastor is, how can we be sure that we are truly called to pastoral ministry? How can we be certain that we are serving in God's power and calling and not our own? Let's take some time to consider the nature of God's call to spiritual leadership and the evidences of that call being worked out in a minister's life.

Defining God's Call to Pastoral Ministry

The New Testament uses the word "call" in three unique ways. In 1 Corinthians 1 we find all three of God's calls and see each one's distinguishing mark and purpose.

The call to pastoral ministry is not the first call a potential leader receives. The first call a leader must receive is God's *call to salvation*: "God is faithful, by whom you were called into the fellowship of his Son, Jesus Christ our Lord" (1 Corinthians 1:9). A pastor must be truly born again and alive in Christ before God can ever use him to lead others.

It may sound strange, but sometimes people who are not saved find their way into church leadership. For them the ministry is a career choice that gives them social status or financial return.

I pastored a large church in Canada for nineteen years, during which time I watched a national church denomination slide into theological liberalism. This national church identified itself as Christian, yet in 1997 the denomination's national moderator declared that the divinity of Jesus and the realities of heaven and hell were irrelevant, tersely saying, "I don't believe Jesus was God, but I'm no theologian."[1] In the wake of this departure from sound doctrine, one of the preaching pastors of this national church became disenchanted with the doctrinal changes and started attending our church. After attending for a few months, this pastor asked to see me personally. At our meeting he confided in me that he did not personally know Jesus Christ as his Savior! He was a professional pastor but not a personal believer in Jesus.

More than once in my pastoral ministry I have personally led a career pastor to answer God's call to salvation. The Bible strongly warns us, "Examine yourselves, to see whether you are in the faith. Test yourselves. Or do you not realize this about yourselves, that Jesus Christ is in you?—unless indeed you fail to meet the test" (2 Corinthians 13:5)! The first and foremost call to all church leaders is God's call to salvation.

Next, a godly leader called to pastoral ministry must embrace the *call to sanctification*: "Those sanctified in Christ Jesus" He "called to be his holy people" (1 Corinthians 1:2, NIV). Genuine saving faith in the Lord Jesus motivates a pastoral leader to accept the lifelong call of living a holy life. God's call to pastors is a call to holiness.

Leaders who do not pursue a holy life forfeit God's blessing. Many leaders are disqualified from fruitful ministry because they disregard or discount the priority of personal holiness. Every Christian leader needs to remember that nothing is hidden from God's sight and that at the judgment seat of Christ, God will expose every hidden motive: "Do not pronounce judgment before the time, before the Lord comes, who will bring to light the things now hidden in darkness and will disclose the purposes of the heart. Then each one will receive his commendation from God" (1 Corinthians 4:5). "If anyone cleanses himself from what is dishonorable, he will be a vessel for honorable use, set apart as holy, useful to the master of the house, ready for every good work" (2 Timothy 2:21). Pastors are not perfect people, but they must continually answer God's call to sanctification and pursue a holy life.

The third biblical call is God's *call to serve*. We see this modeled in the life of Paul, as he was "called by the will of God to be an apostle of Christ Jesus" (1 Corinthians 1:1). Paul's call to apostolic leadership did not come from Paul. He consistently saw this call as a gift that he had received from God and a stewardship to be completed for God. Paul's call to serve the Lord originated by the will of God (see Romans 1:1; 1 Timothy 1:1).

Paul's experience is typical of the pastors God uses. Great spiritual leaders understand that they did not set a goal to become a leader but rather responded to God's call to serve. Consequently, it is mandatory that Christian leaders hear and answer God's call rather than seeking out a position for personal reasons. This high and holy call to serve God as a pastor is the foundation of a leader's effectiveness, authenticity, courage, and perseverance in times of trial.

I have often said of my role as a pastor, "If this is a job, I quit. But it's not a job, it's a calling from God, and I cannot quit on God, because God will never quit on me." The call of God to serve as a pastoral leader is the basis of divine authority and fruitfulness in ministry.

Think It Over: Defining God's Call to Pastoral Ministry

1. What are the three distinct calls of God to anyone in leadership?
2. In what order do God's three calls come? Why is that order significant?
3. Have you answered God's first call to salvation? When? How? Why?
4. What evidence demonstrates that you are pursuing holiness in your life and ministry?
5. What are some practical ways a pastor can serve his flock?
6. Have you heard God's call to pastoral ministry?
7. How can you be sure that pastoral ministry is God's call for you and not just a personal goal or a job?

Discerning God's Call to Pastoral Ministry

God calls *unlikely* people to His service: "I am God, and there is no other; I am God, and there is none like me, . . . calling . . . the man of my counsel from a far country" (Isaiah 46:9–11). But how does a person know whether he himself is called or not? In almost every case in Scripture, God's special leader felt personal reservations about aspiring to leadership, but as each one considered God's call, the Lord confirmed His will and purpose for that person's life and ministry.

Moses initially questioned God's wisdom in choosing him to lead Israel. He struggled with God about his fitness for leadership. Unwilling to answer God's call, Moses repeatedly asked God to excuse him from the call to lead for two reasons. First, he feared that enslaved Israel would not accept him as a qualified leader, and second, Moses battled with the personal embarrassment of stuttering (see Exodus 3–4).

Similarly, when God called Gideon, God knew that Gideon didn't see himself as a leader. Gideon was shocked when the angel of the Lord appeared to him. He had been hiding from the Midianites inside a winepress, fearfully threshing out a few handfuls of grain (see Judges 6:11). The angel of the Lord called Gideon a "mighty man of valor," even though Gideon looked like anything but a courageous leader.

But in time God's called man was given a new identity with a new name, Jerubbaal, meaning "contender of Baal" (see Judges 7:1). God's call moved Gideon toward the Lord's high purposes. With his new identity, Gideon was given a courageous leadership role that had seemed impossible when he was first called. In the same way, Moses was strengthened and helped by God's insistent call, and despite his fears and objections, he went forth to lead Israel out of slavery and to the Promised Land.

The call of God to an unlikely man is also found in the life of David. When God called David to be king over Israel, David's father Jesse did not consider his youngest son a candidate for royal service.

The prophet Samuel had asked seven of Jesse's sons to parade past him so that he could see which one would be anointed king:

> When they came, he looked on Eliab and thought, "Surely the Lord's anointed is before him." But the Lord said to Samuel, "Do not look on his appearance or on the height of his stature, because I have rejected him. For the Lord sees not as man sees: man looks on the outward appearance, but the Lord looks on the heart." Then Jesse called Abinadab and made him pass before Samuel. And he said, "Neither has the Lord chosen this one." Then Jesse made Shammah pass by. And he said, "Neither has the Lord chosen this one." And Jesse made seven of his sons pass before Samuel. And Samuel said to Jesse, "The Lord has not chosen these." Then Samuel said to Jesse, "Are all your sons here?" And he said, "There remains yet the youngest, but behold, he is keeping the sheep." And Samuel said to Jesse, "Send and get him, for we will not sit down till he comes here." And he sent and brought him in. Now he was ruddy and had beautiful eyes and was handsome. And the Lord said, "Arise, anoint him, for this is he." (1 Samuel 16:6–12)

David's father did not believe that David was qualified, so he left him in the field tending the sheep. In his father's eyes David was too young, too busy with lesser things, and too insignificant to be compared to his brothers. How could God use a young shepherd? But despite his father's lack of confidence in him, David was God's choice. When Samuel saw David, the Lord told the prophet, "'Arise, anoint him, for this is he.' Then Samuel took the horn of oil and anointed him in the midst of his brothers. And the Spirit of the Lord rushed upon David from that day forward" (1 Samuel 16:12–13). When God's call came to David, the young shepherd appeared the most unlikely of Jesse's sons, proving that God calls leaders by His sovereign grace and not according to human calculation.

In the New Testament we discover the same principle at work. Even the most prominent church leaders had shortcomings, flaws, and personal inadequacies. However, God saw the potential of His grace and power working in and through these people, and He called them to become transformational leaders.

On the Day of Pentecost, for example, we read in Acts 2 that God clearly called Peter to boldly preach the gospel. However, just weeks before this, following Christ's resurrection, Peter had been a broken man filled with remorse for his three denials of Christ at the Lord's trial. In John 21 we find Peter in the presence of the risen Christ feeling totally inadequate to answer Jesus' call to serve His flock. Then, in a private conversation over breakfast on the shores of Galilee, Jesus distinctly asked Peter three times if he loved Him. Peter answered Jesus all three times, confessing his affection for Christ, and with each answer, Jesus boldly called Peter to lead the flock of God.

It seems odd that Jesus would call such a known failure to such an enormous task. However, God's call is never contingent upon previous failures or on a person's past performance but on the indwelling power of the Holy Spirit. Jesus did not call Peter to lead until He called Peter to love Him. This is the first and foremost prerequisite for Jesus' call to leadership: "Do you love Me?" With Peter's love for Jesus reconfirmed and the promise of the coming Holy Spirit, Peter went on to become the most courageous preacher imaginable and an apostle with a reputation for boldness. Those who love Jesus are qualified to answer God's call, and those God calls He also equips and empowers.

Sometimes God calls natural leaders who are unlikely because of their pride. Saul of Tarsus was a confident and gifted leader with exceptional qualifications (see 2 Corinthians 11:16–22). But even with his natural talents and gifting, no one would ever have guessed that he would become the apostle Paul, the greatest missionary for Jesus Christ to the Gentiles in the Roman Empire. As a former blasphemer and persecutor of the church of

Jesus Christ, Paul did not seem to be the kind of leader whom God would use to lead the Gentile world to Jesus Christ. However, after his encounter with the risen Christ, Paul saw himself as "called by the will of God to be an apostle of Christ Jesus" (1 Corinthians 1:1).

Once God called him, Paul proved to be a force that would change the world. He recognized the miraculous nature of God's call when he said, "I received mercy because I had acted ignorantly in unbelief, and the grace of our Lord overflowed for me with the faith and love that are in Christ Jesus" (1 Timothy 1:13–14). Paul understood that God's call was not based on his natural leadership gifts but on the basis of God's grace and mercy.

After God called Paul, He did employ Paul's natural leadership skills in His service, but that is not why God called Paul. God's call to spiritual leadership is always a gift that flows out of the grace of Jesus Christ: "Grace was given to each one of us according to the measure of Christ's gift" (Ephesians 4:7). No one has ever earned God's call through natural gifting. It comes by the unmerited favor of Jesus. Spiritual leaders are chosen by the grace of God, not on the basis of natural talents.

The circumstances surrounding a leader's call may vary, but God's call is always the same. It is not primarily about natural aptitude or the lack of it; it is always about the sovereign choice of God and the unlimited power of God released in the life of a man. The prophet Jeremiah gave Baruch wise counsel when he said, "Do you seek great things *for yourself*? Seek them not" (Jeremiah 45:5). Answering God's call is never about seeking greatness for oneself but about humbly seeking to serve God in God's way, with God's power, for God's purpose, motivated by God's love to reflect God's glory.

Think It Over: Discerning God's Call to Pastoral Ministry

1. What does the fact that God uses unlikely people to lead say about Him?
2. In what ways do you consider yourself to be an unlikely leader?
3. Describe your own experience of God's call using the questions "when," "how," "who," "where," and "why."
4. What do you find to be irresistible about your call?

God's Call Will Always Be Tested

Human ambition might be applauded in the world, but it causes the death of spiritual leadership within the church. The apostle Paul knew little of the kind of prestige and respect that is given to many Christian leaders today. Instead, he faced great dangers, constant persecution, and the burdensome responsibility of the churches. His reward for leading the church was to be tested by hunger, imprisonment, hardship, and many more tribulations (see 2 Corinthians 11:23–33).

When these difficult and perilous times tested Paul, he always remembered that his call had not been his own idea. He had been called *by the will of God* and not out of his own yearning. By contrast, counterfeit spiritual leaders are filled with proud ambition and have little appetite for hardship or strenuous assignments. A true spiritual leader must understand the risk involved in following God's call. Here is the reason why: every person God calls, God tests: "I the Lord search the heart and *test* the mind, to give every man according to his ways, according to the fruit of his deeds" (Jeremiah 17:10).

God promised Abraham a son, and by faith Abraham believed God's word, but God tested Abraham's faith by requiring him to wait many years for his son and then later by asking him to offer Isaac on an altar. God called Moses to lead Israel out of slavery, and then God tested Moses by having him lead the people for forty years in the wilderness. Paul believed that God had called him to preach the gospel in Rome, but God tested Paul by sending him to Rome as a prisoner rather than as a preacher. Answering God's call to lead the church is the most important work in the world, but leaders must never see it as self-promotion. Eventually God tests everyone's call with adversity—and the hour of testing can be endured when a leader knows that he is called of God. To endure the storm every leader must be able to return to God's call and not to personal ambition as the basis of spiritual leadership.

In times of severe crisis, a pastoral leader may waver and start to question his call. If he perseveres through the wilderness of testing, he will discover that in such times a leader can learn valuable lessons that make him a far better leader.

I was called to lead a seeker-driven church, where I followed a pastor who had specialized in what many described as "motivational talks" and "feel-good" sermons. On my first Sunday, I preached directly from the Bible and publicly called unbelievers to place their faith in Jesus. The spiritually starved flock loved the direct, persuasive, and loving sermons from the Bible, but the church elders objected to it on the grounds that preaching from the Bible so boldly might offend someone. Apart from the elders' objections, however, everyone could see that God was blessing the preaching of His Word. The once-stagnant church was quickly flooded with new believers, new members, and new financial support, and we were able to build new buildings.

After a year of fresh growth, the elders called me into a secret meeting and informed me that I was immediately released as lead pastor. They cited no reason other than that I was not a good fit. My sudden departure came as an unwelcome shock to the congregation and a devastating blow to me. To cover their alarmingly unpopular decision, the board leadership cast doubt on my reputation to the congregation. They told the people, "We cannot talk about the reasons why Jerry is not fit for this job."

In the wake of their action and cover-up, I was deeply hurt, my reputation unjustly tarnished, and my family deeply disillusioned. I wondered if I could go on in ministry. God was testing my call.

Days later some dear friends came to comfort me, and I told them that I questioned whether God wanted me to go on in ministry. In a moment of deep pain, I said, "The very thing that God taught me to love I now hate." My hurt overwhelmed me.

During this time of testing my wife encouraged me with these wise words: "They can take away your job and try to ruin your ministry reputation, but they can never take away who you are!" I will never forget those words! They were like a cascade of fresh water in my emotional desert. With her encouragement my wife reassured me that unfair circumstances never eradicate God's call.

As time passed, I came to understand the powerful truth of her words. God used the testing of my call to prepare me to be a more godly pastor and a better leader for my next calling: the birthing of Cornerstone Church in Long Beach, California, which He raised up to become a world-changing church. (See appendix 1 for a list of things I learned during my time of testing.)

When a Christian leader is fully confident that his call to leadership is from God, he will remain faithful, even when tests come. Jesus contrasted the difference between a hired hand and the good shepherd: when trouble or opposition comes, the hired hand flees, but the good shepherd continues to faithfully care for the sheep (see John 10:11–13).

Think It Over: God's Call Will Always Be Tested

1. How has God tested your call?
2. What have you learned from the tests you have endured?

God's Call Is Irresistible

When God's call comes to us, it is as if an irresistible duty and powerful motivation move in and capture our heart. The prophet Jeremiah testified to an inner fire that he could not extinguish: "If I say, 'I will not mention him, or speak any more in his name,' there is in my heart as it were a burning fire shut up in my bones, and I am weary with holding it in, and I cannot" (Jeremiah 20:9). God does not give uncertain calls or change His mind. God's call comes with an unmistakable conviction that He is compelling us to take leadership to accomplish a specific task.

Jeremiah was called to preach a difficult message of God's coming judgment to a rebellious nation. Such an assignment would not have been possible for Jeremiah without a clear sense of God's call. This is why it is often said, "If you can avoid entering the ministry, do so! If you can do something else, do it." A called leader must believe that saying yes to God is the *only thing* that he can do and the one thing that he *must* do. This is what separates an anointed spiritual leader from those who look for a position.

God's anointed leaders live with a driving inner motivation to serve God and obey Him at all costs. This is why great leaders work with such a high level of enthusiasm and devotion. The fire within them will not die until they have accomplished the task that God has given them to do. Count Nikolaus Zinzendorf (1700–1760), the leader of the Moravian church, relinquished his royal position and material wealth to bring the gospel to millions. He summed up his burning ambition in one phrase: "I have one passion; it is He, He alone."

Think It Over: God's Call Is Irresistible

1. How has God irresistibly convinced you of His call to pastoral ministry?
2. What task burns in your heart that you feel compelled to do for the Lord?

God's Call Is to Serve Others

God's call is a path to greatness of a different kind than that which the world seeks. True greatness in God's kingdom is not found by scaling the ladder of success; it is found by descending to the level of a servant. Leadership greatness does not use position or authority as a means of advancing an agenda or getting help. Greatness is found in humbly sacrificing oneself in the service of others.

Jesus established a new standard of leadership excellence when He said,

> You know that those who are considered rulers of the Gentiles lord it over them, and their great ones exercise authority over them. But it shall not be so among you. But whoever would be great among you must be your servant, and whoever would be first among you must be slave of all. For even the Son of Man came not to be served but to serve, and to give his life as a ransom for many. (Mark 10:42–45)

One of the key words that Jesus used to make His point is "over." Lording it *over* others or exercising authority *over* others describes the methodology and motivation of worldly leaders. Spiritual leadership and true greatness move in the opposite direction. The spiritual leader descends to greatness by serving others as Jesus did. The Lord's leadership greatness is described this way: Jesus "emptied himself, by taking the form of a servant" (Philippians 2:7), and He gave His life "as a ransom for many" (Mark 10:45). Jesus put the needs of other people first and gave up His life to redeem the lost.

While Jesus deserves and receives all praise in heaven, His motivation in the incarnation was not to use His high position or title as the Son of God to have others serve Him. Jesus humbled Himself, taking on the form of a servant. Similarly, God calls His servants down a difficult path to greatness through humble service to others.

Such service is never without a cost. It comes as the result of many prayers and tears. The ability to serve at this level is granted to those who awake every day to put to death the unholy trinity of me, myself, and I. Servant leadership is the business of those who have surrendered themselves to God's service, have courageously laid down every idol, have embraced the cross, and now run life's race looking to Jesus.

True greatness does not come by advanced degrees, family status, or great achievements. Real significance in God's kingdom comes by counting all things loss for the sake of Christ. It is the humble, servant-hearted leader whom God lifts up and then uses to greatly influence men on Earth, shake the courts of heaven, and storm the gates of hell. It is this kind of person God is looking for. Second Chronicles 16:9 charts God's plan to locate and call such leaders: "The eyes of the Lord run to and fro throughout the whole earth, to give strong support to those whose heart is blameless toward him."

Think It Over: God's Call Is to Serve Others

1. In what ways do you sacrifice yourself and demonstrate genuine care for others?
2. What has serving others cost you, or what might it cost you in the future?

God's Call Needs Church Confirmation

It is not enough for someone to prove his call by claiming to have a certain feeling or citing a dramatic circumstance. The potential for self-deception and self-appointment is so great that God has given a protective measure to confirm a person's call to the ministry: the inward call to spiritual leadership must be confirmed by the practical and outward affirmation of the church.

Consider this biblical example. At his dramatic conversion, Paul knew without any doubt that Jesus had called him to be a missionary to the Gentiles (see Acts 9:10–16). But God had one more step for Paul before he could fulfill his calling: after fasting and prayer, the church leaders in

Antioch recognized the Holy Spirit's call for Paul and Barnabas to be missionaries to the Gentiles (see Acts 13:1–3). God's method of confirming His will was for the church to affirm Paul and Barnabas as leaders to be sent out to take the gospel to the Gentiles. Paul respected the church's observation of his call and gifts.

The same principle of confirmation is seen in the life of Timothy, who, according to Eusebius, was appointed to be the leading pastor in Ephesus.[2] His sincere faith was first seen in his mother and grandmother, but growing up in a godly home was not enough to qualify him. Timothy's giftedness as a young spiritual leader was observed and affirmed by Paul, who encouraged him, "Fan into flame the gift of God, which is in you through the laying on of hands" (2 Timothy 1:6). Timothy received his confirmation from the church when the elders laid their hands on him to confirm God's call (see 1 Timothy 4:14).

When the inner call of God and the outward affirmation of the church match, it is time for a spiritual leader to proceed. This protective measure is God's way of screening those who have a genuine call from those who merely want a job or a church leadership position.

Think It Over: God's Call Needs Church Confirmation

1. In what ways has your call been affirmed by others in the church?
2. If "the inner call of God and the outward affirmation of the church match," is anything holding you back from proceeding in pastoral ministry?

Evidences of God's Call

Once a Christian leader occupies a place of service in the church, four ongoing evidences prove that this leader is operating under the power and provision of God's call.

First, the leader must know that *his gifts and ministry belong to God* who calls and gives the gifts. A godly leader gives credit and glory to God for how God works through him. He never steals God's glory.

First Peter 4:10–11 underscores the fact that God bestows gifts upon us and then gives us grace to exercise those gifts to benefit others, and the ultimate glory for the blessing of the gifts goes to God: "As each has received a gift, use it to serve one another, as good stewards of God's varied grace: whoever speaks, as one who speaks oracles of God; whoever serves, as one who serves by the strength that God supplies—in order that in everything God may be glorified through Jesus Christ." A leader who is operating under the call of God diverts attention away from himself and his giftedness. His sole purpose in ministry is to bring glory to God. This is the first evidence of a genuine call.

Second, the leader who is genuinely called understands that *his words are not his own*. God's leaders do not market their own opinions to impress people or to attract a bigger audience. The called leader speaks with authority derived from the Word of God. Courage to say hard things from the Bible without regard to oneself is a defining mark of a called leader.

Third, a called leader *is not concerned with pleasing men but desires to please God*. The declaration contained in 1 Thessalonians 2:4 is a godly leader's motto: "We speak, not to please man, but to please God who tests our hearts." The ongoing concern of a called leader is neither the appreciation of God's people nor the praise of the world. The final court of affirmation for him is the approval of God. The words "well done" spoken by Jesus at the end of his life will be the greatest reward possible.

Finally, the called leader will give ongoing evidence that *his ministry is done in the power and strength of God*. "Whoever serves [should do it] as one who serves by the strength that God supplies" (1 Peter 4:11). The shallow well of human effort might appear to be fresh and deep enough, but in a short time that well runs dry and turns bitter. Leaders whose ministries last over time and have eternal impact are those who rely on the empowerment of the Holy Spirit.

Think It Over: Evidences of God's Call

1. How do your current life and ministry confirm the genuineness of your call?
2. As a minister, do you ever seek to bring attention to yourself, or is your primary passion to bring glory to God?
3. What hard things have you had to say or might you have to say as a minister in our day and age?
4. How can you ensure that you remain dependent on the Holy Spirit in your role as a pastor?

CONCLUSION:
The Pastoral Leader and the Call to Ministry

My maternal grandfather answered the call of God to be a pastor when he owned a department store and was mayor of his town, and he left behind his wealth and position to answer God's call. Years later when he heard that I too was answering God's call to the ministry, he said, "If God has called Jerry, it will be the most blessed life possible." My grandfather was right. Answering the call of God to humbly serve Jesus, my Savior and Lord, has given me the greatest life. I am humbly grateful that God graciously called me to His service.

God's call is awesome to behold and to personally experience. God is searching for leaders to call, to equip, and to send out to do His will. May every man whom God has called to pastoral ministry know the certainty of God's call, be strengthened and established in his call, and prove the call through evidences of God's power and pleasure in and through his ministry.

2

The Pastoral Leader's Qualifying Character

***Objective:** To list and explain the biblical character traits of a pastor using a simple and easy-to-understand method and provide an evaluative tool that will enable church leaders to determine who is qualified to take pastoral leadership in the church.*

Spiritual leadership demands godly character. A leader's godliness is far more important than his natural talent, giftedness, or skill; spiritual leadership transcends the power of personality and all natural talents.

Christlike character is the moral currency of every spiritual leader. A surgeon may be admired for his charismatic personality, but when a person needs lifesaving surgery, he needs a doctor who didn't cheat on his exams. In the same way, the church needs godly leaders who are authentic and empowered by the Holy Spirit. A deceptively unrighteous leader may initially appear successful in the eyes of men, but over time his moral poverty will become known. One of the greatest illustrations of this controlling principle is seen in the contrast between King Saul and King David. At the beginning of Saul's reign, the kingdom of Israel appeared to be in good hands. Saul had a striking physical presence and the enthusiastic support of an adoring nation that longed for a king. But over time Saul demonstrated an evil tendency to reject God's clear instructions. His hidden flaws were uncovered in his disobedience to God at Gilgal (see 1 Samuel 15), his murderous jealousy of David (see 1 Samuel 18–19), and his desperate consorting with the witch at En-dor (see 1 Samuel 28). His proud and stubborn character cost Saul the throne and eventually caused his tragic suicide.

David, on the other hand, "followed [God] with all his heart" (1 Kings 14:8). He entrusted his call to kingship into God's hands and allowed God to fight his battles for him, and he refused to wreak vengeance on Saul, despite Saul's ongoing attempts to vilify and murder him (see 1 Samuel 24). The result was that the kingdom was firmly established in David's hands by God Himself (see 2 Samuel 5:1–5). (See more on the comparison between Saul and David in appendix 2.)

The Lord is not impressed with outward appearances: "The Lord sees not as man sees: man looks on the outward appearance, but the Lord looks on the heart'" (1 Samuel 16:7). Church leaders who are naturally handsome or charming must never believe that their appearance or charisma is their ticket to success in the ministry. If a leader is tempted to believe that he is the reason for any success he enjoys, he must think again. Jesus warned, "Woe to you, when all people speak well of you, for so their fathers did to the false prophets" (Luke 6:26). What should matter most to a leader is how he looks to God. Those who make internal godliness and Christian virtue their first priority will be qualified to lead in God's kingdom.

Godly character is essential because a leader is called to *set an example* for the flock under his care. Paul stressed this to Timothy in 1 Timothy 4:15–16: "Practice these things, immerse yourself in them, *so that all may see your progress.* Keep a close watch on yourself and on the teaching. Persist in this, for by so doing you will save both yourself and your hearers." It is not enough for a leader to *tell* his congregation that believers ought to be Christlike; a pastor must *live a life of godliness* through consistent practice.

The best leaders constantly pursue a deeper relationship with Christ, as Paul did: "Not that I have already obtained this or am already perfect, but I press on . . . toward the goal for the prize of the upward call of God in Christ Jesus" (Philippians 3:12–14). People are only too ready to put their pastor or leader on a pedestal—that is a danger. A pastor must make sure that everyone he leads knows that he has not arrived but is growing in his relationship with Jesus Christ.

Setting an example of moral vigilance and doctrinal purity is vital to leading others in the church. Given enough time, every leader will either provide a tragic Saul-like example or a godly David-like example for others to follow.

The best picture we have of leading by example is our Lord Jesus Christ. For three years Jesus trained His disciples by teaching them and providing them a living example to follow. Jesus made His leadership strategy clear when He said, "A disciple is not above his teacher, but everyone when he is fully trained will be like his teacher" (Luke 6:40).

In Jesus' leadership training school, the disciples heard Jesus pray, teach, preach, and converse as they walked together with Him. They witnessed Him eating, sleeping, performing miracles, boldly confronting His critics, and touching children with tenderness. Many times Jesus took His disciples aside to reveal the secrets behind His ministry (see, for example, Matthew 13:36–43).

The importance of a leader living an exemplary life led James to warn against becoming a teacher, because "we who teach will be judged with greater strictness" (James 3:1). Peter also taught that the primary responsibility of leaders is to be "examples to the flock" (1 Peter 5:3). When a leader suffers a moral or doctrinal failure, it infects believers with discouragement and division, and it also affects those outside the church by causing the credibility of the faith to suffer. This is why Paul instructed Timothy, "Keep a close watch on yourself and on the teaching. Persist in this, for by so doing you will save both yourself and your hearers" (1 Timothy 4:16). The motto of every spiritual leader should be these words of Paul: "Be imitators of me, as I am of Christ" (1 Corinthians 11:1).

So what specific character traits does God look for in His leaders? If God were taking job applications for pastors, who should apply? The Bible lays out the pattern for a pastoral leader's qualifying character in Paul's two letters to Timothy and his letter to Titus. The qualifying traits of spiritual leadership fall into five basic areas outlined in 1 Timothy 4:12: "Set the believers an example *in speech, in conduct, in love, in faith, in purity*." These five aspects of godly character form a pattern around which all other qualifications connect.

The Speech of a Pastoral Leader

Paul begins his teaching on a leader's speech by stating that "an overseer must be . . . able to teach" and "able to give instruction in sound doctrine" (1

Timothy 3:2; Titus 1:9). A pastor's speech should evidence an ability to teach and explain the Word of God so that people can understand. Additionally, Paul states that a pastor must not be "quarrelsome" or "double-tongued" (1 Timothy 3:3,8). Pastors are to use their tongues for the high purposes of encouragement, teaching, preaching, prayer, and counsel.

Able to Teach with Sound Doctrine

One of the primary characteristics of a pastor is skill in teaching and preaching. To be an effective teacher, the spiritual leader must communicate sound doctrine with clarity, passion, and love.

The pathway to skillful teaching requires the pastor to be an avid learner and an ongoing student of the Word. Paul's advice to Timothy was, "Do your best to present yourself to God as one approved, a worker who has no need to be ashamed, rightly handling the word of truth" (2 Timothy 2:15). The skillful Bible teacher will know such basics as how the Bible fits together, where major doctrines are articulated, how Jesus is revealed in both Old and New Testaments, how to trace God's plan of salvation through the Bible, and where to find answers for the practical side of Christian living.

But the ability to teach goes beyond verbal skill. Effective teaching is dependent on the character of the teacher. A teacher cannot separate what he says from what he does. In this respect, a critical component of a pastor's teaching is the pastor's life. The able teacher will only be able to teach effectively if he lives up to what he teaches. Therefore, being "able to teach" is a moral qualification as well as a qualifying verbal gift. The consistency of a spiritual leader's speech and life either qualifies or disqualifies him in God's sight.

First Timothy 5:17 adds extra insight to the role of teaching. It says that elders should be "considered worthy of double honor" if they work hard, or "labor," at preaching and teaching. The word Paul uses for "labor" describes a teacher who works to the point of exhaustion in teaching the Word. The scope and depth of the Bible require spiritual leaders to pursue a lifetime of hard work. The pastor who desires to edify his congregation so that the people are equipped to do the work of the ministry must labor hard at feeding them well. The skill of those who are "able to teach" must always be in development. Teaching entails continual honing and sharpening.

A leader who is "able to teach" should never be careless, frivolous, or foolish with words, but this does not mean that a pastor cannot have a sense of humor. In fact, it is necessary for a leader to maintain a keen sense of humor in order to bring balance and a lighter outlook to difficult situations. "A joyful heart is good medicine, but a crushed spirit dries up the bones" (Proverbs 17:22). A leader who brings a joyful heart to his teaching will find that his hearers will be more ready to hear the difficult parts of Scripture.

There is immense life-giving or life-destroying power in the tongue: "Death and life are in the power of the tongue, and those who love it will eat its fruits" (Proverbs 18:21). The Bible is filled with instruction on the use of language. (See a list of Scriptures on this topic in appendix 3.)

Skillful speech builds people, moves people, and transforms people, while lazy or ungrammatical speech is not taken seriously. The words of a godly leader have the potential to lift listeners to the highest eternal purposes and greatest earthly good. If a leader is to say the right things in the right way, he must be the right kind of person by cultivating a godly heart. It's as Jesus said in Matthew 12:34–35: "Out of the abundance of the heart the mouth speaks. The good person out of his good treasure brings forth good." The good leader watches over his heart, because he knows that the heart is directly connected to the mouth.

Not Quarrelsome or Double-Tongued

A pastor should also be self-controlled and restrained (see 1 Timothy 3:2) in his everyday conversation; in other words, moderate in speech and tone. Even when the speech of others is unrestrained and insensitive, the godly leader follows the example of Jesus, whose speech was always true, thoughtful, and kind. Speaking the truth in love eliminates exaggeration and inappropriate emotion.

Qualified leaders should never be "quarrelsome" or "quick-tempered" (see 1 Timothy 3:3; Titus 1:7). Angry men do not accomplish the will of God but instead stir up strife and division. "Whoever is slow to anger is better than the mighty, and he who rules his spirit than he who takes a city" (Proverbs 16:32). Even when anger seems justified, it can quickly turn sinful if the leader does not restrain it. Anger can become sinful and ungodly when a pastor does any of the following:

- Allows an offense to grow greater than it really is
- Dwells on an offense and allows it to foster a bitter attitude
- Looks for ways to get revenge
- Uses his anger to justify condemning others

Paul reminds believers that the only kind of anger that pleases God is a holy anger that leaves no room for sin: "Be angry and do not sin; do not let the sun go down on your anger, and give no opportunity to the devil" (Ephesians 4:26–27). A godly leader is not angry or divisive (see 1 Timothy 3:3), nor does he look for an argument to stir up contention. Leaders who constantly seek to debate others over the smallest issues are typically guilty of using strong emotion to control and exercise power over others. When emotions are at a high pitch, reason or logic will not change a quarrelsome person. It's best to withdraw from an argument with a quiet response than to try to argue and prove someone wrong.

A quarrelsome person uses blame to take advantage of others. To the argumentative leader, a problem is always someone else's fault. This kind of leader finds it difficult to listen to the views of others, because his mind is already made up. Argumentative leaders feel personally threatened and defensive when anyone expresses a view different from theirs. This misuse of strong emotion disqualifies a person from Christian leadership.

Think It Over: The Speech of a Pastoral Leader

1. What specific things can you point to that demonstrate that you are a good student of the Bible? How much time do you spend each day in God's Word?
2. Are you able to share the Word of God in a public group with observable spiritual impact? What growth in the lives of people can you point to because you taught them the Word?
3. Whom have you recently led to trust in Christ as Savior?
4. What major Bible doctrines do you feel confident teaching? In what doctrines would you welcome more growth or learning?
5. Do people like to sit under your teaching or are they distracted or bored? Why?

6. How do you respond when someone personally offends you? Would most people say that you are gracious or judgmental? Why?
7. What can you point to in your life that shows you are a peacemaker?
8. What strategies would you use to divert a quarrel?
9. Are you known as someone who keeps promises and confidences?
10. Are you a truth teller at all times? Do you say one thing publicly and another in private?
11. In what way would you approach a person to say something difficult but truthful?

The Lifestyle of a Pastoral Leader

The Bible teaches that a leader's entire life is his message. Hypocrisy kills a leader's credibility and casts shadows on his message.

Jesus called hypocrisy the "leaven of the Pharisees" (Matthew 16:6), because the Pharisees were quick to instruct others on matters that they themselves didn't follow. Jesus said of these men, "They tie up heavy burdens, hard to bear, and lay them on people's shoulders, but they themselves are not willing to move them with their finger" (Matthew 23:4).

Jesus reserved His strongest rebukes for these religious leaders of His day because they were corrupt on the inside while maintaining a pretense of holiness on the outside: "Woe to you, scribes and Pharisees, hypocrites! For you are like whitewashed tombs, which outwardly appear beautiful, but within are full of dead people's bones and all uncleanness" (Matthew 23:27). Saying the right things in public can never be a cover for doing evil in private. Leading others is serious business, requiring the highest level of self-examination and character building.

Sober-Minded, Self-Controlled, and Disciplined

Paul instructed that leaders should be "sober-minded" and "self-controlled" in 1 Timothy 3:2, and in Titus 1:8 he called them to be "disciplined." The essential quality of self-discipline allows all other natural gifts to flourish. A leader must first conquer himself if he is to conquer the assignments that God has given him.

Sober-mindedness and self-discipline create an environment in which sacrifice and hard work can grow. Too many leaders with great potential drop out of the ministry not because they are insufficiently gifted but because they are undisciplined. Pastors are hindered from being successful when an area of their life is out of control.

Leaders must work at being self-disciplined in order to be effective in the ministry. Disciplined leaders work while others waste time, study when others sleep, and pray while others merely daydream. Disciplined leaders bear fruit.

Not a Drunkard or an Addict

A disqualifying factor for pastoral leadership, according to Paul's list of qualifications, is drunkenness: "An overseer must be above reproach, . . . not a drunkard" (1 Timothy 3:2–3; see also Titus 1:7). Why are the sins of drunkenness and addiction wrong for the spiritual leader?

First, drinking alcohol impairs a leader's ability to think clearly, make decisions, or hear from God—capabilities that church leaders must be able to access at all times. Proverbs says, "It is not for kings to drink wine, or for rulers to take strong drink, lest they drink and forget what has been decreed and pervert the rights of all the afflicted" (Proverbs 31:4–5). A spiritual leader is in a position of authority and decision making, so it is not safe or wise for him to drink alcohol.

Second, drinking wine could cause a weaker brother to stumble in his faith (see 1 Corinthians 8:9). The negative effects of addiction are so devastating that the spiritual leader must never allow wine to be the justification for an addict to fall back into a life of addiction.

Third, drunkenness violates God's command in Ephesians 5:18: "Do not get drunk with wine, for that is debauchery, but be filled with the Spirit." This biblical maxim from Paul is a spiritual leader's guide to wine and many other questionable practices. "'All things are lawful for me,' but not all things are helpful. 'All things are lawful for me,' but I will not be dominated by anything" (1 Corinthians 6:12).

Respectable

The leader's demeanor in the public arena is important. According to Scripture, a leader should be dignified and "respectable" (1 Timothy 3:2). The goal is moral consistency and personal integrity, whether inside the home or outside in public. God's qualified leaders are to be morally upright even when no one is looking.

On the other hand, Christian leaders are not to pretend that they are perfect when they fail. Part of being respectable and humble is admitting failure quickly, turning from it, and learning from it.

One thing that hinders transparency is fear of rejection. Leaders wonder if people will lose respect for them if they find out that they are imperfect. The greatest fear that any leader should have, however, is the fear of hypocrisy. An honest leader was heard saying, "I show my scars so that others will know that they can heal." Respect is gained and not lost when a leader is honest in failure, humble in weakness, and redemptive in recovery.

Not a Lover of Money or Greedy for Gain

The pastor's lifestyle needs to be free from the love of money as his motivation for ministry. Paul warned both Timothy and Titus of this disqualifying trait (see 1 Timothy 3:3; Titus 1:7).

Jesus identified the quest for wealth as a false god that presents itself as a tempting alternative to serving the one true God: "No one can serve two masters, for either he will hate the one and love the other, or he will be devoted to the one and despise the other. You cannot serve God and money" (Matthew 6:24). One of the identifying signs of a false teacher is that he imagines "that godliness is a means of gain" (1 Timothy 6:5). Today's false teachers promoting the prosperity gospel or the health-and-wealth gospel have clouded the true message of the gospel and birthed a body of false teaching that makes a few preachers wealthy at the expense of their followers. The prosperity gospel is greed-based teaching that misleads unsuspecting Christians into believing that God's goal for every believer is material wealth.

Genuine Christian leaders are motivated by their love for God and not a love for money. In 2 Corinthians 5:14 we find every leader's motivation for serving God: "The *love of Christ* controls us, because we have concluded this: that one has died for all." The purest motivation for ministry is a loving response to the unlimited and sacrificial love of Jesus Christ.

Pure and Honorable in Marriage

Another qualifying lifestyle trait of a pastoral leader has to do with his relationship to his wife. A Christian leader may be single like Paul (see

1 Corinthians 7:8) and enjoy being unburdened by the responsibilities of marriage; however, the leader who is married must demonstrate his leadership starting inside his own home.

A pastor is to be "the husband of one wife" (1 Timothy 3:2; Titus 1:6), meaning that he has a reputation of faithfulness to one woman. The emphasis is on fidelity to one wife. This instruction allows a pastor to remarry should his wife die or if he is biblically divorced.

God designed marriage to be the best illustration of Christ's love for the church and the church's submission to Christ (see Ephesians 5:23–24). Therefore, the marriage of the Christian leader must be generously filled with sacrificial love, unconditional forgiveness, and mutual submission.

The Bible does not specifically address the involvement of the pastor's wife in any ministry. In other words, the pastor and his wife determine how active she should be. The main area of responsibility for any wife is to support and be submissive to her husband (see Ephesians 5:22–24). There is no cookie-cutter approach to the role of a pastor's wife. The wife does not do the work of the pastor, but the pastor and his wife are a team yoked together to do God's work. One of the truly remarkable qualities of a pastor's wife is when she is able to show a faithful love for the church members that she and her husband serve.

The Bible does speak to the character of the pastor's spouse, however, saying that wives should "be dignified, not slanderers, but sober-minded, faithful in all things" (1 Timothy 3:11). The pastor's wife can advance or undercut her husband's call to ministry depending on how well she obeys these simple principles.

A wise pastor's wife also helps her husband balance between the ministry and marriage. Too often a pastor can be so busy helping and giving to others that he neglects family life and intimacy with his wife. The picture of Christ and His bride, the church, is a portrait of balance.

The pastor's wife should encourage her husband in making her the love of his life! A pastor needs time to have fun and enjoy his wife to the fullest! A ministry couple needs to make time for small outings together so that they can be alone and away from the pressure of people with needs.

Managing His Household Well

Paul lists a godly family life among the qualifications of a pastor. He says that a leader "must manage his own household well, with all dignity keeping his children submissive, for if someone does not know how to manage his own household, how will he care for God's church?" (1 Timothy 3:4–5; see also 3:12). Paul also writes that a leader's children should be "believers and not open to the charge of debauchery or insubordination" (Titus 1:6).

Raising children within the context of a busy ministry is not easy. It requires a pastor and his wife to work closely together. A leader's ministry aspirations are achievable only when both husband and wife join forces to make their home a little taste of heaven on Earth. Leaders who make home a priority will not do ministry at the expense of the family. Neglect of the family is a trap. A good balance between home and ministry is always an ongoing task.

Pastors face an even more difficult challenge should their grown children leave the home and depart from their Christian faith. Children in the home live under the direct supervision of their parents, and the parents are responsible to see that their children honor the Lord; but this changes when a grown child leaves. If a child leaves home and chooses to rebel, the leader is called upon to manage this heartbreaking disappointment in the same way God handles His children when they disobey Him: "Hear, O heavens, and give ear, O earth; for the Lord has spoken: 'Children have I reared and brought up, but they have rebelled against me'" (Isaiah 1:2). It is comforting to the parents of a wayward child to know that God understands what it is like to have children reject Him and His instruction. If God, who is a perfect parent, had the children of Israel rebel against Him, it is highly possible that a Christian leader, who is an imperfect parent, might have a child rebel against him.

How did God address His rebel children? First He warned them of the disastrous consequences of continuing in a state of rebellion (see Isaiah 1:4–9). Next He lovingly called them to forsake their sin and move back toward Him (see Isaiah 1:10–17). Finally He tenderly offered His rebellious children complete forgiveness and restoration (see Isaiah 1:18–20). This is God's three-step plan for defiant children outside the home—the Christian leader must warn, love, and pray. Then a good parent must be prayerfully patient until the erring child returns to God.

If a leader follows God's pattern of managing a rebel child, he can rest assured that God will be pleased with him. Rather than disqualifying a leader, this kind of test actually proves a leader's ability to remain godly in a difficult personal situation.

Think It Over: The Lifestyle of a Pastoral Leader

1. Would people say that you generally display good common sense and restraint, or are you typically rash or impulsive? Explain.
2. How do you maintain control of your time? Your diet? Your money? Your temper? Your emotions? Your thought life?
3. Do you have any emotional attachments or addictions in your life that are unhealthy? If so, how will you free yourself from them?
4. How are you careful to do nothing that could cause a weaker Christian to stumble?
5. Does your external appearance measure up to what the average person sees as proper, both biblically and culturally? Explain.
6. How does your life demonstrate that you trust God when tested financially?
7. What are your habits when it comes to giving regularly to God? How are you generous with your money?
8. Do you have high moral standards as to what you read and watch (in theaters, on video or DVD, on television, on the Internet)? What measures have you taken or can you take to keep sexual temptation from overtaking you?
9. What are some words that people use to describe your spouse? In what ways do others show respect to your spouse inside and outside the church?
10. How much help do you offer your wife to help her keep your house clean and organized?
11. What are you doing to train your children in godly character? How do your children show respect for you and your words?
12. How do your children behave in public? Do they respect other adults?

The Love of a Pastoral Leader

A pastoral leader should be known first and foremost for his love for God and second for his love for people. A loveless leader is disqualified from leading God's people. Jesus summed up the entire Old Testament law in this way: "The most important [law] is, 'Hear, O Israel: The Lord our God, the Lord is one. And you shall love the Lord your God with all your heart and with all your soul and with all your mind and with all your strength.' The second is this: 'You shall love your neighbor as yourself'" (Mark 12:29–31).

A spiritual leader represents God to the church and to the world. What should the world and the church see? That "God is love" (1 John 4:8). Given this reality, Paul gives several hallmarks related to love that describe godly leaders: they are to be gentle, non-violent, not quick-tempered, hospitable, and lovers of good (see 1 Timothy 3:3; Titus 1:7–8). When Paul described the essential qualities of love in 1 Corinthians 13, he said that love is patient and kind and that it is not easily provoked. When a spiritual leader loves people with God's love, he will draw people to himself and to the Lord.

Gentle, Non-violent, Not Quick-Tempered

A leader filled with the love of God will exercise patience, treat others with gentleness, and never use violence or temper tantrums to solve a problem (see 1 Timothy 3:3). A "quick-tempered" person is not qualified to lead in the church (Titus 1:7).

The Greek word *orgilos* found in Titus 1:7 means "inclined to anger, passionate, cross, irritable, sharp-tongued, short fused." A quick-tempered leader is a dangerous person to follow. "A man of quick temper acts foolishly, and a man of evil devices is hated" (Proverbs 14:17). When rage rules the heart of a leader, almost any foolish thing can happen. A hot-tempered leader may lash out with strong emotion and then play the victim, blame others, or just sulk. This kind of behavior is not worthy of a spiritual leader, who is to be motivated by infinite love of God.

Hospitable

A qualified leader is "hospitable" (Titus 1:8). Hospitable leaders draw people, because they place a high value on relationships. Hospitable leaders make good friends, because they draw the very best out of others.

One of the most beautiful statements that Jesus made to His disciples is the one in which He called them His friends: "No longer do I call you servants, for the servant does not know what his master is doing; but I have called you friends, for all that I have heard from my Father I have made known to you" (John 15:15). A spiritual leader is not an island living in friendless isolation. Leaders should learn to model their friendships after Jesus and His disciples. Jesus befriended those who followed Him, and He revealed His heart to them.

Some leaders believe that they cannot have close friends because they may be judged for showing favoritism. This idea goes against the pattern of Jesus with His disciples. Jesus had an inner circle of Peter, James, and John as His closest friends, then the other nine disciples, the seventy-two (see Luke 10:1), the one hundred twenty (see Acts 1:15), and the rest of those who followed Him. Even God the Son had special friends!

The inevitable consequence of a leader who avoids friendships is a lonely, discouraged, and vulnerable leader. The self-imposed seclusion of inhospitality leads to tragedy. A friendless leader is a failed leader who is a danger to himself and to the church.

Loving What Is Good

Finally, loving leaders should be known for loving what is "good" (Titus 1:8). Godly leaders possess clear moral judgment that acts as an internal compass. They love whatever is good and gravitate toward it, because they know that rightness has the built-in reward of blessing, while evil destroys those who love it. The pastor's conscience is trained by constant practice to distinguish good from evil (see Hebrews 5:14). Leaders love what is good, pure, right, and true and hate what is evil, impure, dishonest, and deceitful. They love what is good, and they *are* good, because they feel deeply grateful for the enormity of God's goodness to them.

It is unrealistic to think that a spiritual leader's circumstances will always be pleasant. At times a leader's life involves bad things such as sickness, hardship, injustice, broken relationships, or death, but those hard facts of life are never to cloud the bright sun of God's goodness. The Bible teaches that God "richly provides us with everything to enjoy" (1 Timothy 6:17), has equipped us "for every good work" (2 Timothy 3:17), has "blessed us in Christ with every spiritual blessing" (Ephesians 1:3), and has promised us that He will bring to completion the good work that He has begun in us (see Philippians 1:6). Good leaders are good because everything about God and His plans is good.

Think It Over: The Love of a Pastoral Leader

1. How do you show kindness and respect toward those who are lowly or financially poor?
2. What are some ways you secure the cooperation of others without using your authority to threaten people?
3. How do you promote peace, harmony, and unity rather than causing division when doctrinal issues are discussed? Can you see the good points in the views of other Christians with whom you generally disagree? Give one example.
4. How do you handle being under authority (in the church, in business, in society)? Do people generally say that you hold your temper well?
5. How quickly do you forgive others who have wronged you? Name someone you have forgiven.
6. How often do you invite people to church? At church meetings do you go out of your way to meet visitors or people you don't know?
7. How do you use your home to minister to people?
8. Would people who know you say that you generally have a cheerful countenance?

The Faith of a Pastoral Leader

Spiritual maturity is a quality necessary to be a good leader; a leader's faith must be proven before he is qualified to lead God's people. He cannot be immature, exhibiting qualities such as arrogance or stubbornness. Instead his character must be informed and shaped by the Word of God. Only when a pastor is spiritually mature will he be able to faithfully teach God's Word and refute error.

Not a Recent Convert

Paul warns the church of the foolish mistake of placing immature believers into leadership, cautioning in 1 Timothy 3:6 that a leader should not be "a recent convert."

An immature Christian should not be pushed into leadership out of desperation to fill a vacant position or because he is accepted as a leader outside the church. Sometimes celebrities who come to faith in Jesus are immediately put into ministry because they're famous. This is equally destructive to the new believer, the watching world, and the church.

Wise parents would never put their toddlers in charge of making dinner over a hot stove, because it would be dangerous for the baby and disastrous for the family. In the same way, if an immature believer is placed into leadership too quickly, there is a real danger that he will become conceited and fall into the devil's trap: pride and self-exaltation. It takes time to develop an understanding of God's Word, come to settled convictions about doctrine, and learn to shepherd people. Jesus' plan for greatness is the path of humble service, and that lesson is not learned in a day.

Even Paul did not appoint leaders in every city he went to on his first missionary journey. Timothy was converted on Paul's first missionary journey but not ordained as a leader until Paul's second missionary journey. Maturity in godliness is a process that must not be hurried.

Must Be Tested

A leader's faith must "be tested first" before he can be trusted to lead God's people (1 Timothy 3:10). This is how God has always prepared His choicest leaders.

God prepared Joseph to lead an entire nation, using a series of trials that required Joseph to patiently trust in Him. God sovereignly placed Joseph in a position of power only after he had passed numerous tests. Following this testing God deemed Joseph prepared to rescue his family from starvation and secure the promise of the coming Messiah.

God tested Moses when he ran from Pharaoh's household to the desert as a fugitive. Eventually Moses became a shepherd of sheep within the confines of his father-in-law's household, and there in the desolation of the desert God deeply tested Moses' character. Acts 7:23 says that Moses was forty years old when he left Egypt, and Acts 7:30 tells us that it was forty years more before the angel called to Moses from the burning bush. God's great task for Moses to lead Israel out of slavery required great testing over a forty-year period.

David was anointed king, but he didn't assume the throne immediately. God tested David with the difficult job of being King Saul's servant, musician, and armor bearer. Again David was tested when he faced Goliath alone on the battlefield. David fought against the Philistines for King Saul, and when he was successful, Saul became so insanely jealous that he tried to kill David. Later David was tested again when he had more than one chance to kill Saul but chose to spare Saul's life. Only after many years with many tests did David finally assume the throne that God had anointed him to occupy.

This principle of leadership preparation through testing runs throughout the Bible. We never find any great leader whom God used who was not first tested. All spiritual leaders must be tested in the shallower waters of troubles and disappointments before God can call them to sail in the deep waters and storms of spiritual leadership.

Not Arrogant or Stubborn

There is no room for an "arrogant," self-willed person in spiritual leadership (Titus 1:7). How is it possible for any God-appointed leader to be arrogant when Jesus is so humble? The humility of Jesus is presented in such astonishing terms in Philippians 2 that it is impossible for us to comprehend it.

The word "arrogant" in Titus 1:7 means to be consumed with self and to stubbornly seek self-satisfaction to the complete disregard of others. An arrogant person is an ego-driven individual who is typically obstinate and uncooperative. In the world's system people look for a strong, aggressive, natural leader. However, God looks for humble leaders who model their leadership style after Jesus, who was a servant leader. The need to be important and to lord it over others does not fit the example of Jesus. Anyone dominated by arrogant self-interest is not fit to be a leader in the church.

Holding Firm to the Word and Refuting False Teaching

It is critically important that the faith of a pastor rest upon the foundation of God's unchanging Word. "He must hold firm to the trustworthy word as taught, so that he may be able to give instruction in sound doctrine and also to rebuke those who contradict it" (Titus 1:9).

A good pastor is precise and careful when speaking on doctrinal matters or delicate issues around which misunderstanding could occur. This means that the leader must have a good understanding of the major doctrines of the Bible so that he can teach with clarity. If a pastor is unsure about doctrine, then it is very likely that his followers will be even more confused. As the old saying goes, "A mist in the pulpit is a fog in the pews."

The leader's faith grows to maturity as he continues to be a learner and a student of God's Word. A mature leader communicates the Christian faith with precision and clarity, relying completely on the Word of God. As Paul told Timothy, "Do your best to present yourself to God as one approved, a worker who has no need to be ashamed, rightly handling the word of truth" (2 Timothy 2:15).

A leader's grasp of sound doctrine should enable him to easily spot false teaching and defend against it. He must be able to rebuke those who contradict the truth. The best way to spot a counterfeit is to know the real thing comprehensively. Confronting false teachers and false doctrine with the truth is a vital qualifying factor of a good leader. Sheep are easily misled, and a good shepherd will keep close watch for deceptive wolves in sheep's clothing.

Think It Over: The Faith of a Pastoral Leader

1. How long have you been a believer?
2. In what ways have you shown proven character in serving in a church ministry?
3. What trials have you faced and succeeded in by trusting in God?
4. Would people around you say that you constantly promote yourself or the things you are doing, or would they say that you are humble?
5. In your opinion, what false doctrines threaten the church today? How would you answer these doctrinal challenges?

The Purity of a Pastoral Leader

The apostle Paul describes the personal moral purity of a spiritual leader as needing to be "above reproach" (1 Timothy 3:2; Titus 1:6). When a pastor is pure and above reproach, it is also likely that he will have good relationships with people outside the church, or "be well thought of by outsiders" (1 Timothy 3:7). Such a man will be "upright" and "holy" (Titus 1:8).

Above Reproach and Blameless

A Christian leader must have a solid reputation without any grounds for unethical accusation. Some Bible translations use the word "blameless" in Titus 1:6 to describe this quality (the NLT, for example). If a leader's personal purity is questionable, then everything else in his life and ministry also comes under question.

After years of counseling pastors who have fallen into sexual sin, one thing stands out to me: sexual immorality is a common temptation. But if a pastor understands this hazard, he will be careful to avoid it. So what must a pastor know about remaining sexually pure?

First, a pastor must *fully understand the relationship between his occupation and his vulnerability to temptation*. Various circumstances contribute to sexual indiscretion, but the root problem is the pastor's own vulnerability to sin. Spiritual and sexual maturity requires that pastors "put to death therefore what is earthly in [them]: sexual immorality, impurity, passion, evil desire, and covetousness, which is idolatry" (Colossians 3:5).

While practical measures like Internet filters, avoiding counseling a woman alone, and being deliberate to take one's wife out on special nights may be helpful, they don't completely address the reality of temptation. These practical boundaries look at the problem through the eyes of reason alone. However, sexual temptation does not obey reason.

In the face of temptation, a pastor's thinking can become unpredictable, uncontrollable, and irrational, because the source of temptation is the heart. This is what Jesus taught: "Out of the heart come evil thoughts, murder, adultery, sexual immorality, theft, false witness, slander" (Matthew 15:19). If the life of God indwelling the pastor does not rule his heart, then sin will dominate him. Failure to put to death the sins of the old nature creates one of the greatest dangers to the servant of God. Lose this battle, and a leader could lose not just the spiritual battle within but also his purity, his marriage, and his leadership in the church.

Second, every spiritual leader must *avoid the occupational hazard of being placed on a pedestal*. The more public a pastor's ministry becomes and the more esteemed his preaching is, the more dangerous and effective will be the devil's schemes toward him. A pastor who finds satisfaction in self rather than in the glory of God becomes dangerously proud and vulnerable to personal failure. This is a deadly poison. Pride breeds a sense of entitlement that ultimately destroys a ministry and a pastor's life.

Along with arrogance comes a dependence on natural abilities, gifts, and accomplishments; an unguarded leader allows these to feed his soul more than the Word of God does. These circumstances form a trap that can engage a pastor in risky thoughts and behaviors. The pride that comes with being on a pedestal causes a pastor to believe that he is beyond danger and can get away with what he is doing. The Bible warns that pride goes before a fall (see Proverbs 16:18). That is true for leaders and followers alike.

Third, the pastor who desires to maintain purity must *fully understand how some relationships can be hazardous*. The pastorate can be a lonely place when a pastor does not tend to his internal emotional needs. Working too many hours can lead to the neglect of a pastor's wife and family. Emotional need grows unanswered, leaving the pastor vulnerable. In such a scenario, an admiring woman with a compliment for the pastor and a need for attention can create a powerful temptation. This door leads to destruction. A pastor seeking purity should know that his wife's evaluation of him as a man is the only one that counts.

Given this potentially disqualifying hazard in ministry, a pastor needs to take deliberate steps to avoid being caught in this web of consuming desire and destruction. First, I strongly recommend that every pastor *memorize 1 Corinthians 6:18–20* and use it often:

> Flee from sexual immorality. Every other sin a person commits is outside the body, but the sexually immoral person sins against his own body. Or do you not know that your body is a temple of the Holy Spirit within you, whom you have from God? You are not your own, for you were bought with a price. So glorify God in your body.

Second, every leader must *pray a prayer* like this: "Lord, keep me from sexual sin, even when I am too foolish to keep myself." The Bible tells believers to "put no confidence in the flesh" (Philippians 3:3). Complete trust in God to deliver from sexual sin is essential.

Third, every leader needs to *have an accountability friend or group of mature male believers* to air his struggles. To be sexually mature, we must be spiritually mature, and to be spiritually mature, we must be sexually mature. In other words, we must not separate our sexuality from our spirituality nor our spirituality from our sexuality. Prevention is possible when we recognize that everything we do in ministry relationally and sexually must point to one purpose: the glory of God.

Having a Good Reputation with Outsiders, Upright

Another of Paul's qualifications for a pastor is that "he must be well thought of by outsiders" (1 Timothy 3:7). Such a leader will also be, as Paul wrote to Titus, "upright" (Titus 1:8).

The reputation of a Christian leader outside the church is either like an open door that welcomes unbelievers to investigate the gospel or a closed door that says to the unbeliever, "Danger! Keep out!" Some ways to build a good reputation with those outside the church are to offer community service, show concern for the poor, and build relationships with civic and educational leaders. An upright leader is just, fair, and righteous in human relationships. Such a leader will be able to make sound judgments and act with the highest intention.

Holy

The final description on the biblical list of a pure leader is "holy" (Titus 1:8). A holy leader is a man whose heart is pleasing to God. His internal devotion to the Lord will lead to observable practical holiness on the outside. A holy leader is a blessing to his followers. Everyone knows that a holy leader keeps promises, is on time, does not deviate from complete honesty, and can be trusted not to break a confidence.

Think It Over: The Purity of a Pastoral Leader

1. How do those closest to you (your wife, other church members) feel about your qualifications to be an elder?
2. To whom are you open and vulnerable about your personal life?
3. Are you completely honest in your business dealings with those in your community? How would your neighbors describe you?

4. Who seeks you out as a wise and fair counselor?
5. Why do you desire to please God more than men?
6. Are you living free of any habitual sins? If not, how will you address the sin in your life?
7. How would you describe your prayer life? How will you build a stronger prayer life?

CONCLUSION:
The Pastoral Leader's Qualifying Character

It is no surprise that the qualified spiritual leader described in 1 Timothy 3 and Titus 1 has a wide range of qualifying traits that are a mirror image of the character of Christ. In Acts 11:26 we read that believers "were first called Christians" in Antioch. The pagans of Antioch actually created the name "Christian" as a mockery because those who followed Jesus were so much like Him.

In a similar way, when people outside the church interact with a qualified Christian leader, they may not agree with him or choose to follow him, but they will know that they have been with someone who is like Jesus. This is the ultimate qualification for any spiritual leader—to love like Jesus and thus lead like Jesus!

3

The Pastoral Leader's Personal Life

***Objective:** To provide the pastoral leader with instruction on how to keep himself in top mental, physical, and spiritual condition and define the potential temptations and pitfalls that could destroy a leader.*

To say that an extraordinary life is required of a pastor is not an exaggeration. The church leader is expected to have a growing spiritual life, necessary spiritual gifts, complementary natural talents, a good mind, the capacity to develop healthy relationships, the ability to avoid temptation, a vigorous physical constitution, and effective management skills. Having an abundance of these gifts and abilities separates pastors who barely survive from pastors who excel.

It is often stated that Paul was the most fruitful missionary of the first century. We find convincing reasons for this: Paul came from a solid family, had a keen mind, was highly educated, was naturally talented, built good relationships, understood how to manage people, was physically vigorous, and was completely devoted to Christ and His cause (see Acts 22:3; 2 Corinthians 11:21–29). Yet Paul realized that if his personal life became unfocused or undisciplined, his ministry would be finished:

> Do you not know that in a race all the runners run, but only one receives the prize? So run that you may obtain it. Every athlete exercises self-control in all things. They do it to receive a perishable wreath, but we an imperishable. So I do not run aimlessly; I do

> not box as one beating the air. But I discipline my body and keep it under control, lest after preaching to others I myself should be disqualified. (1 Corinthians 9:24–27)

What runner would choose to enter a race if he knew that he would be disqualified before he reached the finish line? The logic for a pastor is the same: what pastor would enter into leadership if he knew that he would fail by his own carelessness or be told to step down in shame? What leader would purposely embarrass himself this way? The three goals of every spiritual leader should be to be faithful, to be fruitful, and to finish well. At the end of his life, Paul could honestly say, "I have fought the good fight, I have finished the race, I have kept the faith" (2 Timothy 4:7).

What can a leader do to prepare his life to run the race and keep himself strong enough to finish well? The place to start is the leader's private life.

A Pastoral Leader's Spiritual Life

Everyone knows that a person cannot draw water from an empty well. But a pastor who does not keep his relationship with God fresh attempts to do exactly that. He reaches down into his natural talents or his charismatic personality or relies on his position or privileges to do his ministry. That is a recipe for disaster.

The prophet Jeremiah spoke against the leaders of his day and the futility of their self-empowered efforts: "My people have committed two evils: they have forsaken me, the fountain of living waters, and hewed out cisterns for themselves, broken cisterns that can hold no water" (Jeremiah 2:13). A cistern is a container designed to catch and hold water. In this verse God rebuked Israel for two ways in which they had disobeyed Him: first, they had forsaken Him, the true God and the fountain of living water, and second, they were trying to refresh themselves using their own containers instead of relying on Him. Leaders who attempt to draw water from their own resources will discover that it is like trying to draw water from a dry well.

It's like this: God says to the leader, "I am the living water, and it's available to you in communion with Me." Yet the self-sufficient pastor says, "No thanks, God! I appreciate the offer, but I see a shovel over there. Think I'll dig my own cistern!" What happens to spiritual leaders who think that they can get by on their own talents and personality without tapping into a living relationship with Jesus Christ? Their cisterns of personal talents and human strength always break; they never hold water. The leader remains thirsty, unable to quench his own thirst or offer water to others who are spiritually thirsty.

God wants His leaders to talk to Him in daily prayer. A pastor's prayer life needs to be intimate, honest, and open to God's leading. God wants His leaders to read His Word to water and grow their own soul, not just to plan another lesson or sermon. God wants the pastor to fill up on Him, the living water. God wants to quench the thirst in His leader's life before He can use the leader to minister to others. God wants the leader to readjust his perspective on his life and to seek the spring of living water in order to grow spiritually.

Digging our own cistern will never satisfy. It's not meant to. Broken cisterns cannot hold water. And to top it off, God will never help us dig our own cistern. We get angry when it seems as if God won't help us, but it's often because we're shoveling as fast as we can to dig our own well. God will never help us seek joy and spiritual vitality outside Himself.

To keep a fresh relationship with God, a leader must do several things:

- Pray for his life and his personal needs daily.
- Confess any sins immediately and turn from them.
- Invest time daily in reading the Bible, asking God to reveal Himself and His will.
- Worship God in private by adoring Him and singing to Him.
- Welcome personal growth and change with each passing year of ministry.
- Pray routinely for the filling and empowerment of the Holy Spirit.

The demands of the ministry can drain a pastor dry, so going to the fountain of living water in times of stress is crucial. Sometimes the struggles within us or the circumstances surrounding us will cause us to feel spiritually dry. When you hit a dry period, do not attempt to dig your own cistern. You will only dig yourself into an empty pit and a dark, depressing place. Keep seeking God in all His fullness, and rest in His sufficiency to keep you fresh and growing.

Think It Over: A Pastoral Leader's Spiritual life

1. On a scale of one to ten, with one being bone dry and ten representing an overflowing spiritual life, where would you rate yourself in your relationship to God right now?
2. What factors have contributed to where you are spiritually?
3. How much time do you spend each day seeking God through His Word and prayer?
4. How much time would you like to spend alone with God? What's keeping you from doing so?
5. Examine your life against the bulleted list in the section above to see how fresh your relationship is with God. What is missing that you need to add to your life?
6. What other practices to help keep you fresh spiritually could you add to the list?

A Pastoral Leader's Giftedness

Every pastor who is truly called of God already has the gifts of pastoring and teaching. Those are the pastor's primary gifts, because they relate to his function within the church, the body of Christ (see chapters 6 and 9 in this book). A spiritual leader may have other spiritual gifts as well, and he will also have natural talents that make him unique.

It is crucial that a pastor know the spiritual gifts and natural talents that God has invested into his life. A leader can develop a God-given spiritual gift or natural talent, but he will be frustrated trying to develop a gift or talent that he does not have. For example, some pastors would like to be able to sing, but God didn't give them a beautiful singing voice. It is a waste of time to try to develop a singing voice when God has given that talent to another person.

Assessment tools can help uncover each pastor's unique God-given mix. I recommend the *Design* workbook that I authored based on Wayne Cordeiro's book *Doing Church as a Team* because it includes assessments of a believer's personal passions, personality type, and spiritual gifts and talents.[1] Once a pastor has determined his God-given design, then he can get ready to develop what God has given him. Personal development is a leader's lifelong pursuit. Every gift and talent can be developed through training, education, practice, and evaluation.

A leader needs to constantly ask himself four questions:

1. In what ways can I improve my skill or performance? Where am I lacking in understanding, skill, confidence, and effectiveness?
2. What additional training, mentoring, and experience do I need in order to improve?
3. Where can I go to get the training? What resources do I need to obtain? Who best models the gift or talent that I want to improve?
4. When will I start?

Some pastors may decide to return to school to earn an advanced degree, while most will find it best to attend seminars specific to their developmental goals. Every pastor, however, needs to make a commitment to ongoing personal development. Leading is like rowing a boat against the current—once a person stops rowing, he starts slipping backward. A pastor should never put personal growth off but should make a commitment to develop his gifts and skills on an ongoing basis.

Think It Over: A Pastoral Leader's Giftedness

1. What are your spiritual gifts? How do you know?
2. What passions are at the top of your list of things that motivate you?
3. List your talents. How are you using them in ministry?
4. In what ways can you improve your skills or performance? Where are you lacking in confidence and effectiveness?
5. What additional training, mentoring, and experience do you need to improve?
6. Where can you go to get training? What resources do you need to obtain?
7. When will you start?
8. What's your next step?

A Pastoral Leader's Family Relationships

Building and maintaining strong family relationships is at the heart of being a leader. Pastors, like everyone else, depend on their family relationships to help them remain emotionally healthy.

God said from the beginning that it was "not good that the man should be alone" (Genesis 2:18). Jesus didn't call His disciples merely to use them to fulfill His plans; Jesus first called them to relationship with *Himself*: "Follow *me*, and I will make you fishers of men" (Matthew 4:19). Only then did He give them their mission. A pastor always needs to remember that relationships matter more than duties. People are God's plan.

The most important relationships that need a pastor's attention are those with his own wife and children. Healthy home and family relationships provide the emotional security that pastors and their families need.

A pastor's relationship to his wife is critical to his personal happiness and ministry success. A leader's wife needs to feel her husband's love and care and a sense of value before she can flourish in her role as his wife. To keep a healthy marriage, pastors need to plan both time alone and time together with their wives. Healthy pastors celebrate God's gift of a good wife and ministry partner, and they show their love to their wives continuously.

When children come along, a pastor must remember that his children need him first as their dad and not as their pastor. Children born into a pastor's household did not ask for the busy life of a leader. They didn't receive a divine call to be in the ministry. A pastor will keep healthy relationships with his children if he remembers several things.

First, *ministry is people*. A pastor should surround his children with wonderful people, friends, and mentors, introducing them to visiting Christian leaders and letting them be around church leaders, volunteers, interns, and staff. If a pastor's children are young and need a babysitter, an older couple in the church can become "adopted" grandparents who will babysit them with love. Children ought to be influenced by a community of great people.

Second, *ministry means presence*. Flex your church calendar so that you can be at home with your children in the evenings. When our children were young, I made a commitment to always be home for dinner each evening. Only after spending dinnertime with my family did I go to a church meeting at night. Make use of the flexibility of a ministry schedule to be at your kids' school and sports activities. Ministry keeps a pastor busy, but if you take time to be present with your children when they are growing up, when they are older, they will enjoy being present with you, whether at home or in the ministry.

Third, *ministry has perks*. From the time our children were very young, my wife, Sue, always taught our children that serving God is a privilege. We involved our kids in the good parts of our ministry. Our kids went with us to camps, retreats, and other fun events where other children didn't go. As a pastor, look for the good side of serving the Lord and communicate that to your children. Otherwise your children could grow up to resent the church.

And finally, *ministry is not performance*. Allow your children to be themselves. Pastors' kids feel expectations placed on them from people within the church and sometimes from their parents. Pastors teach that every believer should be the unique person whom God created him or her to be, but too often pastors' kids are expected to be what the pastor or the church congregation wants them to be. Focus on your children's relationship to Jesus. He will guide, protect, teach, and lead them and open doors for them. One more thing—keep a sense of humor around the household. Children need to see their parents laugh.

Think It Over: A Pastoral Leader's Family Relationships

1. How would your wife describe your marriage?
   a. Boring but tolerable
   b. Full of duties but no fun
   c. Just getting through the day
   d. Exciting and fresh
   e. Full of love and companionship
   f. Distant and strained
   g. Broken but still together
   h. Other ______________________________
2. What are you doing to get closer to each of your children?
3. Are your children proud of you as the pastor, or do they resent being the preacher's child? Explain.
4. What are some of the advantages to being in your family that your children can point to?

A Pastoral Leader's Temptations

Pastors are not perfect people; they experience the same temptations that every believer faces. Quickly confessing any known sin keeps the leader's spiritual life refreshed. However, some sins have the potential to wreak havoc on a spiritual leader—these sins need to be avoided.

When someone rises to the position of a leader, it is tempting to become *prideful*. Pride can give a pastor a false sense of being infallible and indispensible. If this attitude is not stopped, it will stop the pastor from advancing in God's kingdom, because "the Lord detests all the proud of heart. Be sure of this: They will not go unpunished" (Proverbs 16:5, NIV). Spiritual leaders do not have a position; they have a divine appointment. A pastor should avoid talking about his accomplishments or his responsibilities; instead, he should take James's advice: "Humble yourselves before the Lord, and he will exalt you" (James 4:10), turning people's attention away from himself and pointing them to God. A pastor should also be honest about his shortcomings; doing so will take the sword of criticism out of his opponent's hand.

When things in the ministry don't go as a pastor expects or or when people disappoint, it can be easy to get *angry*. Anger is a strong emotion, and it should be reserved for rare occasions when there is righteous justification for it. Anger is not easily hidden; when a pastor is angry, people can sense it in how he leads and what he says. Remember, "the anger of man does not produce the righteousness of God" (James 1:20). A pastor must take his anger and frustration to God in prayer. He must work out the issues he has with people using good conflict-resolution skills. It is important for a leader to resolve anger quickly, because, left to simmer, anger will give birth to a root of bitterness within.

Because leaders are typically out in front of their followers, from time to time, they will feel *impatient* with how things are progressing. A pastor must be careful not to allow his schedule or expectations to preempt God's timing. Impatience can be a sign of a lack of faith in God's plan and purposes being fulfilled in God's time. King Saul grew impatient when the prophet Samuel didn't show up on schedule. God withdrew His hand of blessing from Saul and removed him and his house from the throne because of this impatience that gave rise to disobedience (see 1 Samuel 13:8–14).

A pastor must avoid *impurity* at all costs. Purity is a prerequisite for intimacy with God. When a pastor keeps his life pure, he will be empowered with the pleasure and the presence of God (see Psalm 24:3–5). Two aspects of purity are required for all spiritual leaders: moral purity and purity of motivation.

Moral purity, as we saw in the previous chapter of this book, is necessary for a pastor to remain in the ministry. The public position of a leader and Satan's desire to disqualify those who lead make moral purity an ongoing challenge.

God also desires His leaders to be pure in motive. God cares more about why His people are doing something good than about what good deed they are doing. The church at Ephesus in Revelation 2 did many right things, and Jesus said, "I know your works, your toil and your patient endurance, and how you cannot bear with those who are evil" (Revelation 2:2). But although it was doing good deeds, the church had abandoned the right motivation for doing well: their first love of Jesus. Therefore Jesus warned them that their lamp stand would be removed—in other words, the power and impact of their church would be canceled. God cares about a pastor's motivation for being a leader and doing ministry. A pastoral leader must let his motivation always be to glorify God in all things: "Whatever you do, do all to the glory of God" (1 Corinthians 10:31).

One of the most damaging temptations that pastors face is thinking that church ministry is superior to family life at home, which often leads to *family neglect*. The Bible gives three qualifying characteristics for an elder that relate to the home: a leader must be the husband of one wife, manage his household well, and have children who are believers. What the leader leaves undone at home can easily unravel the good he does at church. A pastor needs to balance his home life and ministry carefully to avoid family neglect. David was appointed as God's choice to be king over God's people, but his son Absalom showed David the damage that happens when home is neglected (see 2 Samuel 15).

Another sin pastors must guard against is *abuse of authority*. A pastor has been granted limited and delegated authority over plans and people. Disqualification can come when the pastor takes privileges or assumes powers that do not belong to him. The apostle Paul could have exerted his authority many times as an apostle, but he chose to exercise his authority through his service to the church.

Paul speaks of his authority as an apostle in 1 Corinthians 10–13. From these chapters we can glean six principles from the life of Paul on the use of authority in the church:

- Spiritual authority comes through service (see 1 Corinthians 10:14–15). The faith of those in Corinth and the existence of the congregation there were clearly due to Paul's missionary call—his true apostleship as a "sent one." However, Paul did not use his role as founding leader to exercise authority.
- Spiritual authority is exercised without exacting a price (see 1 Corinthians 11:7–9). Paul ministered without charge so as not to be a burden to the congregation.
- Spiritual authority grows through sacrifice, not position (see 1 Corinthians 11:22–28). Paul reluctantly yet boldly described his credentials and his sufferings for the cause of Christ.
- Spiritual authority is not a goal to be sought but a stewardship to be carefully nourished (see 1 Corinthians 11:30–12:10). All spiritual authority and power ultimately come from God.
- Paul said that the signs, wonders, and miracles of a true apostle were performed among the believers, indicating that the credit went to God and to the Holy Spirit rather than to himself (see 1 Corinthians 12:12).
- Authority in the church is delegated and temporary, not absolute or permanent (see 1 Corinthians 13:10). Paul concludes by clearly stating that his apostolic authority was given to him by the Lord for the purpose of building up the church.

A pastor can easily be tempted to get too wrapped up in either *personal success or fear of failure*. The pastor who lives for popularity and people's applause will discover that the pendulum of popularity can quickly swing in either direction depending on circumstances.

Sometimes a pastor is tempted to be jealous of another pastor's success in ministry. How should a leader handle this common temptation? When Eldad and Medad were prophesying in the Israelite camp, Moses could have listened to Joshua, who said, "'My lord Moses, stop them.' But Moses said to him, 'Are you jealous for my sake? Would that all the Lord's people were prophets, that the Lord would put his Spirit on them'" (Numbers 11:28–29). Leaders need to be careful not to fall into the trap of seeing their ministry through the eyes of either adoring followers or harsh critics. Relinquish your ministry success entirely to the Lord, and let His words "Well done" be your goal.

Finally, a pastor must be careful to avoid the trap of *materialism*. The lure of money and the things and power that it can give have taken too many pastors down the road to disqualification in God's sight. The danger of this temptation is found in every one of the qualifying passages for pastoral leaders: "An overseer must be . . . not a lover of money" (1 Timothy 3:2–3) and not "greedy for gain" (Titus 1:7), and he must "shepherd the flock of God . . . not for shameful gain" (1 Peter 5:2). The prosperity gospel being preached by false teachers makes some preachers rich at the expense of their followers. This false teaching is only a cover for rancorous greed and cannot be supported by Scripture. If personal wealth is the sign of success in ministry, then Jesus and Paul were complete failures!

Think It Over: A Pastoral Leader's Temptations

1. Look at the various temptations listed in this section and put them in the order of how tempting they are to you.
2. What two temptations are at the top of your list?
3. Why do you think that these two are the most tempting to you?
4. What is your plan to stay morally pure?
5. What is your plan to stay motivationally pure?
6. What kinds of things upset you most quickly and cause you to feel angry?
7. Have you forgiven everyone who has offended you?
8. When another pastor or a friend has more success than you do, what is your reaction?
    a. I applaud them and praise God for their success.
    b. I ignore them; I don't want to talk about their success, because it makes me feel like a failure.
    c. I belittle their success and try to find reasons why they didn't deserve it.

d. I secretly hope they fail.
e. Other ______________________.

A Pastoral Leader's Mental Fitness

Mental acuity is a biblical mandate for pastors. It may come as a surprise to some spiritual leaders, but God commanded His leaders to sharpen their minds:

> You shall love the Lord your God with all your heart and with all your soul and with all your *mind* and with all your strength. (Mark 12:30)

> Those who live according to the flesh set their *minds* on the things of the flesh, but those who live according to the Spirit set their *minds* on the things of the Spirit. (Romans 8:5)

> Be renewed in the spirit of your *minds.* (Ephesians 4:23)

> Prepare your *minds* for action. (1 Peter 1:13, NASB)

Some practical ways that a pastor can keep his mind sharp and ready for ministry are to get enough rest, eat nutritionally balanced foods, get physical exercise, and challenge his brain with new tasks. Reading and taking part in seminars and educational opportunities are helpful as well. Meditation and prayer will clear a leader's mind and enable him to focus his mind on God's will.

Our minds matter to God, but we must take the responsibility to advance our understanding and mental acuity by continuous learning.

Think It Over: A Pastoral Leader's Mental Fitness

1. Describe your sleep patterns. Do you need to get better rest?
2. What foods help you feel mentally agile? What foods drag you down mentally?
3. What new book, skill, or habit pattern are you working on?
4. During what time of day do you feel most mentally alert?

5. Why does God choose to use those who are mentally ready?
6. What are some reasons that sloppy thinking is not God's will for you?

A Pastoral Leader's Physical Fitness

The pastor's weekly ministry requires him to be physically fit to do it well. Preaching takes a surprisingly large amount of mental and physical energy. Dealing with the spiritual and emotional problems of a flock can load up emotions. Leaders who want to stay healthy must have a physical outlet to express frustrations. Many pastors suffer emotional burnout because they do not attend to their physical body. Set aside time three times a week to get some physical exercise. Medical doctors recommend good physical fitness and proper nutrition because they know they will add up to ten healthier years to our lives. "Your body is a temple of the Holy Spirit" (1 Corinthians 6:19). Keep it in shape.

Think It Over: A Pastoral Leader's Physical Fitness

1. What exercise routine do you currently use? If you don't have one, what is a routine that you would like to use?
2. What part of your body needs the most strengthening and toning?
3. Does a heavy exercise routine reduce stress and feelings of frustration in you?
4. Do you feel stressed? What part of your ministry causes you the most frustration?
5. Do you believe that exercise can help calm your body and lift your frustrations? Why or why not?
6. When will you start your exercise routine? Set a regular time and place.

A Pastoral Leader's Finances

The pastor is called upon to teach biblical stewardship of time, talent, and money. But if the pastor is not a good steward of his own resources, how will his people follow his example? Jesus spoke more about finances and material possessions than He did about heaven, yet many pastors neglect to teach on the subject of stewardship.

I received an easy financial plan from my maternal grandfather, who left the world of business to answer God's call to be a pastor. I call it the 10-10-80 plan. It is a simple financial plan to remember and also to start. Here is how it works:

- Understand that everything belongs to God but that He has put you in charge of a limited portion (see Psalm 24:1–2; Haggai 2:8; Matthew 24:45; 25:14–30).
- You will give an account to God for your exercise of stewardship (see Matthew 25:19; Luke 16:1–2; 8–9).
- God cannot put you in charge of spiritual riches until you have been obedient in material riches (see Luke 16:10–12).
- You cannot love money and God at the same time (see Luke 16:13).

Therefore:

- Give your first 10 percent to the Lord as a tithe (see Malachi 3:8–10; Matthew 22:21).
- Invest or save the second 10 percent for yourself and your family's future (see Proverbs 13:11, 22; 21:20).
- Live on the other 80 percent for your everyday needs (see Philippians 4:10–13,19).

My firm belief, based on God's promises and on my own experience, is that if you follow the 10-10-80 plan, you can expect three results: First, as a tither, you can expect the Lord's blessing on our finances. Second, as a saver and investor of 10 percent, you can expect that you will have enough money to care for yourself in old age. Third, as a careful steward of the 80 percent, you will have enough to provide for your daily needs. With this basic stewardship plan, you will be able to support the work of God, care for your needs, and care for yourself and your family when you grow old.

Think It Over: A Pastoral Leader's Finances

1. Make a list of all your assets and liabilities. What do you own? What do you owe?
2. If you are living with overwhelming bills and debt, what sacrifices will you make to reduce your debt and pay off your bills?
3. What do you think of the 10-10-80 plan? Are you willing to trust God and give it a try?
4. Do you tithe? Read and claim God's promise in Malachi 3:8–10.
5. What investments can you make that have minimum risk and maximum benefit?
6. Do you pray over your finances? What are some specific financial needs that you currently have that you can pray about?
7. What financial plan do you have for when you are too old to work full-time?

CONCLUSION:
The Pastoral Leader's Personal Life

The performance of a leader rests on his ability to leverage, harness, and balance his gifts and abilities under the leading and power of the Holy Spirit. Leaders are not immune from the weaknesses and temptations that wreck lives; if a pastor does not pay attention to his personal development and discipline, then even if he is among the most gifted and talented of leaders, he will be disqualified. But if by adequate preparation and constant vigilance a pastor grows spiritually, mentally, and physically, he will be protected from many dangers and well-equipped to lead God's people.

4

The Pastoral Leader as an Inspiring Trailblazer

Objective: *To give a biblical basis for powerful leadership and explain how a pastoral leader can become a frontrunner who inspires his flock by using a seven-step plan from the life of Nehemiah.*

God is searching for bold, inspired leaders, people with whom He can entrust His greatest work—the building of His kingdom on Earth. Jesus guaranteed success in this greatest of all ventures when He said, "I will build my church, and the gates of hell shall not prevail against it" (Matthew 16:18). The world looks for better methods and more sophisticated technologies, but God is looking for better leaders—believers with godly character and tenacious vision.

Consider what God says about His search for leaders:

The Lord has sought out a man after his own heart. (1 Samuel 13:14)

I sought for a man among them who should build up the wall and stand in the breach before me for the land, that I should not destroy it, but I found none. (Ezekiel 22:30)

I am God, and there is no other; I am God, and there is none like me, declaring the end from the beginning and from ancient times things not yet done, saying, "My counsel shall stand, and I will

> accomplish all my purpose," calling a bird of prey from the east, the man of my counsel from a far country. (Isaiah 46:9–11)

> The eyes of the Lord run to and fro throughout the whole earth, to give strong support to those whose heart is blameless toward him. (2 Chronicles 16:9)

> Jesus looked at them and said, "With man it is impossible, but not with God. For all things are possible with God." (Mark 10:27)

> I am the vine; you are the branches. Whoever abides in me and I in him, he it is that bears much fruit, for apart from me you can do nothing. . . . If you abide in me, and my words abide in you, ask whatever you wish, and it will be done for you. (John 15:5–7)

The Bible demonstrates that when God finds anyone who is ready to fully trust Him, He will do great things through that person and use him to reshape the world. Examples abound in the Bible. Moses, for example, was a fugitive living in a remote desert place when he reluctantly accepted God's call to shepherd Israel out of slavery in Egypt to their inheritance in the Promised Land. Acts 7:35–36 tells us how God used Moses despite his past failures: "This Moses, whom they [the Israelites] rejected, saying, 'Who made you a ruler and a judge?'—this man God sent as both ruler and redeemer by the hand of the angel who appeared to him in the bush. This man led them out, performing wonders and signs in Egypt." God had great plans to change the world through Moses.

It is said that the famous nineteenth-century evangelist D. L. Moody said, "The world has yet to see what God will do with a man who is fully committed to Him." Then he said, "Lord, let me be that man!" But inspirational leaders like Moses or D. L. Moody are rare. Does the challenge of being a great leader interest you? What will it take for you to become a world changer for God?

In the story of Nehemiah, we find seven steps on the path to becoming a trailblazing leader whom God will use. These steps can be easily remembered using the acrostic INSPIRE. You can inspire the world and fulfill God's glorious purposes by learning and practicing these seven steps from the life of Nehemiah.

Intercede to Know God's Will—Prayer

Every great work of God begins with prayer. Seeking God earnestly must be the first step in any challenging journey of faith—especially one that looks impossible.

Nehemiah was an exile in the foreign land of Persia, "in Susa the citadel," serving as cupbearer to King Artaxerxes I, when he received the news that the walls of Jerusalem had been broken down and the gates burned with fire (see Nehemiah 1:1–3,11). Upon hearing that the holy city lay in ruins, Nehemiah fell down, wept, and began to fast and pray. Nehemiah began his earnest prayer for God's forgiveness and Israel's restoration, recorded in Nehemiah 1:5–11, by looking to God who keeps His covenants.

Prayer that has the power to change the world comes from inspirational leaders who allow their hearts to be broken by the human tragedy around them. For decades God had warned the people of Judah that unless they turned from their sins, God's judgment would come upon them—and it finally did. In the aftermath of a foreign invasion and the destruction of Jerusalem, the Israelites of Nehemiah's time were living in the wreckage of their national sins and stubborn rebellion. Jerusalem lay in ruins, the people lived in fear, and hopelessness crippled their will to rebuild. They felt powerless to rebuild their city or their lives, so they gave up and settled into despair. Situations like this are the very circumstances in which prayer can start a movement. When the impossible mocks men, inspirational leaders begin to pray.

Powerful, world-changing prayer always claims the covenant promises of God over human tragedy. Prayer that takes hold of God's promises forms the foundation for miraculous change. Nehemiah's prayer began with his honest admission as to why the tragedy had happened: Nehemiah confessed the sins of Israel, because he knew that Israel's sinful rebellion was the reason that their once-great nation had forfeited God's blessing.

Our world today is in spiritual, social, and economic ruins because of sin. But God is ready to use inspired leaders who start miraculous change through prayer—inspirational leaders who understand that sin devastates people, cities, and nations.

After Nehemiah fasted and prayed, God began to move in a miraculous way. One day in the palace, King Artaxerxes inquired as to why Nehemiah looked so sad. Who had prompted the king to notice and care about Nehemiah's sad countenance? God had! When the king heard that Nehemiah was grief-stricken about the ruins of Jerusalem, Artaxerxes offered to send Nehemiah, with royal building materials, to rebuild the city! God answered Nehemiah's prayer above anything that he could have asked or imagined. This is what I call an Ephesians 3:20 moment, when God "is able to do far more abundantly than all that we ask or think, according to the power at work within us."

This is how God still works when He finds a leader who prays and earnestly seeks His will. The inspired leader who intercedes and does not give up praying and fasting until God's will is known discovers that God acts in powerful ways beyond his original request.

Think It Over: Intercede to Know God's Will—Prayer

1. When you look at the needs around you, what burdens you most about people's broken spiritual and social condition?
2. When you intercede for the needs of people around you, what insights does God give you on how to address people's problems?
3. What are the common sins that have brought on the brokenness that you see?
4. What time are you willing to commit to prayer over these things?
5. Are you ready to identify yourself with the problems and open to God using you to address them?

Never Allow Doubt to Dominate—Discipline

Any great movement of God will come up against difficult moments in which the original task will appear to be stalled or in jeopardy. Many leaders want to see great things happen immediately, but when doubts or negative circumstances overwhelm them, they give up.

Once Nehemiah returned to Jerusalem, he inspected the damage to the city and then marshaled the people to rebuild. They responded enthusiastically, saying, "Let us rise up and build" (Nehemiah 2:18). At that point in the story, everything seemed to be moving in the right direction. God's leader had God's plan, he had the resources to rebuild, and he had the enthusiastic agreement of the people to help him with the job. But just when it seemed that nothing or no one could stand in the way of progress, a devastating challenge arose: "When Sanballat the Horonite and Tobiah the Ammonite servant and Geshem the Arab heard of it, they jeered at us and despised us and said, 'What is this thing that you are doing? Are you rebelling against the king?'"(Nehemiah 2:19). These pagan noblemen living in Jerusalem were threatened by the positive changes that Nehemiah was bringing to the ruined city, so they publicly mocked his plan and showed contempt for the workers. Later they increased their campaign of opposition by spreading a false rumor about Nehemiah, accusing him of treason to King Artaxerxes.

When God begins to do something great, the Lord's work and His workers will not go unopposed. There will always be critics who find fault with a godly goal. If they cannot completely stop the work, they will belittle the workers and threaten the leader with lies and distortion. How does an inspiring leader handle critics who throw mockery, suspicion, and doubt into a situation?

A godly leader will not let doubt dominate his thinking or the thinking of his followers. Exercising faith for a brief moment is not enough to change the world. Nehemiah didn't stop working. He stayed on task in a *disciplined* manner and answered his critics clearly and convincingly: "The God of heaven will make us prosper, and we his servants will arise and build, but you have no portion or right or claim in Jerusalem" (Nehemiah 2:20). Inspiring leaders show courage and faith in the middle of a challenge. They refuse to let doubt undermine what God has shown them in prayer and through miraculous intervention. Inspiring leaders never doubt on the darkest days what God has shown them in the light.

Think It Over: Never Allow Doubt to Dominate—Discipline

1. What barriers to ministry stand in your way? People? Circumstances? Lack of resources?
2. What fears keep you from making yourself available to be God's instrument?
3. How would your faith be tested if you moved ahead despite the obstacles?

See a Better Future—Vision

The inspiring leader should always remember that in order to succeed, he must have a clear vision of the ministry God has called him to do so that he can keep that goal in front of the people he is serving at all times.

When Nehemiah first inspected the debris of the ruined city, the Bible says that he had to dismount from his horse to pass through the mess (see Nehemiah 2:14). The wreckage and rubble that Nehemiah saw that first night would have made anyone sad and depressed. But Nehemiah knew that nothing spoils a godly vision faster than looking at the status quo. Someone has humorously said that the words "status quo" are Latin for "the mess we are in." Messes are not awe-inspiring; they tend to make people feel uneasy and defeated. However, a vision that is from God is exciting and invigorating. Godly vision makes the heart beat faster and causes the mind to imagine how much better everything will be when the vision that God has given becomes a reality.

When Nehemiah walked through the ruins of Jerusalem that first night, he saw not the mess but the new city that God saw, and that is the vision that he would bring before the people of Israel.

God is the Master who changes messes into miracles. Many well-meaning church leaders do not know God's vision for their church or community. It is actually estimated that fewer than one in ten pastors can articulate a vision for their church. Consequently, these pastors have little impact on their congregation or the people in society around them. This may explain why some Christians feel frustrated and disorientated in their church—they do not have any vision from the pastor about where the church is heading.

Nehemiah received from God a vision to use his life to rebuild the walls and gates of the holy city. He could have succumbed to the much easier life of staying inside the palace as the king's cupbearer. Had Nehemiah stayed in Susa, his life would have been luxurious. Instead he accepted God's vision for him to rebuild Jerusalem, which was surrounded by enemies. What Nehemiah saw was not his plan but God's greater vision for his life and the lives of others.

Great leaders are great in part because they understand the spiritual significance of their times. They draw back the curtain of time and glimpse the eternal issues at stake. The holy city of Jerusalem lay in ruins, and God's chosen people were living in defeat. The vision that motivated Nehemiah was simply "what [his] God had put into [his] heart to do for Jerusalem" (Nehemiah 2:12). Inspiring leaders must be able to look ahead and see the end results of the vision God has given them. Responsible leaders always look far ahead and see how their plans and policies will affect future generations. Once an inspiring leader has seen God's vision, he keeps it front and center in his heart and in the hearts of those whom he leads.

Every spiritual leader needs to understand that the people he leads will never go further than the leader's vision. In my life and ministry I have at times attempted new things that seemed so risky that they could only be accomplished if God stepped in. But that's exactly where God intends His leaders to be—in a place of total dependence on Him! Attempt something so big that it will require God to intervene.

When God wants to do something great, He always starts the same way. He finds a leader and puts him in an impossible situation. Then God does something miraculous so that when the vision is complete, God gets the glory!

Vision has a powerful five-way impact on the church:

- Vision builds morale. "Where there is no prophetic vision the people cast off restraint" (Proverbs 29:18). Maintenance mode does not motivate people.
- Vision reduces frustration. "The life of a man of divided loyalty will reveal instability at every turn" (James 1:8, Phillips).
- Vision allows focus and concentration. Paul said, "I am bringing all my energies to bear on this one thing: Forgetting the past and looking forward to what lies ahead" (Philippians 3:13, TLB). The church that forgets the ultimate and important things quickly becomes the slave of immediate and insignificant things.
- Vision attracts cooperation. Paul thanked the church at Philippi because of their "partnership in the gospel from the first day until now" (Philippians 1:5). People gather around exciting vision. They want to be part of something bigger than themselves.
- Vision assists in evaluation. "Examine yourselves, to see whether you are in the faith. Test yourselves" (2 Corinthians 13:5).

> Famous management consultant Peter Drucker was best known for five main questions: What is your mission? Who is your customer? What does your customer value? What results do you seek? What is your plan?[1]

Not every vision I have attempted has been successful, but one thing is certain: without a new vision for God, a pastor will never lead anything new or great.

Think It Over: See a Better Future—Vision

1. What has God shown you that He would like to do for the broken lives around you?
2. What would it look like if God's purposes were perfectly done for these people?
3. What is the brightest part of what you see God doing in the future?
4. What has God shown you that is so clear and powerful that you cannot rest until it is done?

Passionately Communicate the Vision—Zeal

Imagine if Nehemiah had witnessed God's miraculous answer to his prayer, been given all the resources necessary to succeed, and arrived in Jerusalem and seen the potential for a rebuilt city—but had kept silent about it! Someone might say, "What a tragic waste of a great vision!" Saying nothing about his vision would have been a tragedy, and Nehemiah would not have gone down in history as an inspiring leader.

The Bible records that Nehemiah communicated God's vision with zeal to both his workers and his enemies. One cannot help but feel the fiery passion behind Nehemiah's words to his critics: "The God of heaven will make us prosper, and we his servants will arise and build, but you have no portion or right or claim in Jerusalem" (Nehemiah 2:20). In the face of his opponents, Nehemiah restated God's vision to arise and build, and then he boldly and shamelessly excluded his foes from the completion of God's glorious plan to rebuild Jerusalem.

Days later, when the construction of the new walls was progressing well, the same critics gathered sympathizers to their cause. They marshaled a well-armed militia and threatened to invade the city to stop the work. When Nehemiah heard about this planned invasion by the enemies of God's vision, he prayed urgently, "Hear, O our God, for we are despised. Turn back their taunt on their own heads and give them up to be plundered in a land where they are captives. Do not cover their guilt, and let not their sin be blotted out from your sight, for they have provoked you to anger in the presence of the builders" (Nehemiah 4:4–5). As an inspiring leader, Nehemiah continued his prayer life by turning his bold prayers to the protection of God's plan and the punishing of his critics. Zeal for the vision that God had given Nehemiah prompted him to do battle in the highest realm of prayer. His enemies felt the power and purity of Nehemiah's passionate communication with them in bold confrontation and with God in bold prayer.

An inspiring leader understands that his followers must understand and embrace vision with the same zeal that their leader has. Nehemiah's persuasive passion for God's vision came out in his first speech to the beleaguered residents of Jerusalem:

> I said to them, "You see the trouble we are in, how Jerusalem lies in ruins with its gates burned. Come, let us build the wall of Jerusalem, that we may no longer suffer derision." And I told them of the hand of my God that had been upon me for good, and also of the words that the king had spoken to me. And they said, "Let us rise up and build." So they strengthened their hands for the good work. (Nehemiah 2:17–18)

Nehemiah began his passionate address by painting the dark picture of the ruined city and how unacceptable this state of affairs was to God, to him, and to his hearers. He called the situation a mockery and a source of public ridicule. Ancient cities without walls or gates were unprotected and vulnerable to attack by marauding bands of terrorists. Living in an unprotected city made family life and commerce uncertain, scary, and dangerous. After pointing out the problem, Nehemiah motivated the people of Jerusalem by zealously telling them the story of how God had miraculously intervened in the situation. Nehemiah told the people how God had moved the mighty king of Persia to release Nehemiah, his personal cupbearer, to rebuild Jerusalem. Then they heard how King Artaxerxes had given the resources to rebuild the city out of his own royal holdings. Upon hearing of God's miraculous working, the people quickly responded with the passionate answer, "Let us rise up and build."

One of the marks of a great leader is the ability to persuade and motivate his followers. Inspirational leaders know how to paint pictures with words, and with those words they persuasively lay out the need in a way that enables people to see the logic and purpose behind the vision. Then they passionately persuade people to see a brighter future at the vision's fulfillment and, finally, help people see themselves in the vision. The Jews who were living among the ruins of Jerusalem, because of Nehemiah's encouragement, could foresee the time when they would no longer have to suffer the inconvenience of walking through the debris. They could imagine their families living safely behind secure gates and fortified walls. The power to persuade is released when an inspiring leader shows his followers how their lives will be better once the vision is fully realized.

Church leaders who desire God to change their communities and cities must learn to communicate their vision with zeal. To minister effectively and authoritatively, a pastor must first clarify his vision through intercessory prayer, then embrace it and protect it from doubt and doubters, then passionately paint the picture of a better future to those he wishes to lead. Vision is the insight that God provides to enable us to see and follow the pathway He desires us to take. Vision provides the blueprint of what God wants to accomplish through us in building His kingdom. With God's clear vision in hand, both leaders and followers know where they are headed, making the chances of a successful journey guaranteed.

Think It Over: Passionately Communicate What You See—Zeal

1. Whom have you told about the vision God has given you?
2. Who still needs to know about God's vision?
3. What means will you use to communicate that vision?
4. What is your plan to communicate the vision clearly and regularly?
5. When frustrating delays and critics arise, will you have the courage to face them and to passionately defend the vision?

Include Others to Fulfill the Vision—Collaboration

Inspiring leaders tap into the important fact that God designed His people with a desire to be included in things greater and higher than themselves. Christians are powerfully influenced by vision, because God redeemed them to participate in the work He is doing on Earth that will have eternal impact. An inspiring leader understands that God's intentional method is to use His people to complete His redemptive vision for the world.

Nehemiah was a powerful man in the ancient world. As cupbearer to the king of Persia, he was in close personal contact with the king numerous times every day, and as one of the king's most trusted aides, he possessed enormous personal and political clout. However, when Nehemiah was given God's vision for the city of Jerusalem, he did not attempt to complete the mission by himself. Nehemiah wisely used God's people to accomplish God's work.

Nehemiah 3 lists the tribes and clans that were involved in rebuilding the walls and gates. The Bible begins the list of workers with Eliashib, the high priest, and his family. When a big work for God is started, inspirational leaders will discover that the first workers to step up ought to be other leaders, those whose faith is strong and who desire to see God do great things. Inspirational leaders know that people will follow other key leaders in the early going. Finding the opinion shapers in the church and getting them to embrace the vision is crucial to the recruitment of workers.

Nehemiah organized the workers according to tribes and families. Each tribe was assigned a portion of the work according to their skill and giftedness. They worked side by side to get the city walls and gates reconstructed. From the workers' perspective the vision to rebuild was a collaborative and cooperative effort. The vision was big enough to include everyone who had a mind to work.

The completion of a vision from God in the church is never a one-man project. No matter how gifted or influential the leader might be, a great vision needs dedicated workers. Just as in Nehemiah's time, our world today is broken by sin. People live in the ruins of a society that has turned its back on God. A new spiritual vision to change people's lives through the power of the gospel of Jesus Christ is needed today. The Great Commission is Christ's vision for our lost and broken world. Inspirational leaders and those who follow them must passionately communicate the life-changing message of the gospel to a fallen world. God's plan to build the church in our broken world is a harmonious orchestration of every person and every gift and talent:

> By the grace given to me I say to everyone among you not to think of himself more highly than he ought to think, but to think with sober judgment, each according to the measure of faith that God has assigned. For as in one body we have many members, and the members do not all have the same function, so we, though many, are one body in Christ, and individually members one of another. Having gifts that differ according to the grace given to us, let us use them. (Romans 12:3–6)

God calls leaders to mobilize His people to do His work of rebuilding lives and families broken by sin. Each member of the church has been given a measured portion of grace. This means that no one, including a talented leader, can do the work by himself. God's plan is to involve every believer in completing His work on Earth.

Think It Over: Include Others to Fulfill the Vision—Collaboration

1. Have you communicated with the key people who will help you fulfill the vision that God has given you?
2. What plans do you have to help the workers develop ownership of the vision?
3. What kinds of people will you use to get the vision accomplished?
4. How will you divide the responsibilities and the work?
5. Does everyone working on the vision feel a sense of ownership? How can you improve this?

Ruling Wisely in Times of Crisis—Endurance

On the way to the completion of the vision that God had given him, Nehemiah had to endure and manage some messy situations. He faced opposition from outside and discouragement from within. As the work progressed, the threat of attack by enemy armies increased. Because of this, Nehemiah devised a plan to protect the city from invasion while keeping the workers on the job: half the workers continued construction, while the other half stood guard as fully armed soldiers. But just in case of an enemy assault, Nehemiah had the workers keep their weapons close: "Each labored on the work with one hand and held his weapon with the other" (Nehemiah 4:17).

The value of an inspirational leader is understood best when trouble threatens to stop the accomplishment of the vision. In times of crisis leaders demonstrate their endurance and their ability to solve problems. Leaders who inspire people are leaders who walk through crises without caving in.

A young sailor beginning his work with the Coast Guard was assigned to go with his crew into raging seas to rescue a stranded ship. As they began the desperate mission, wind and rain pounded the young sailor's face. In fear he turned to the captain of his ship and cried, "This storm is so big that we'll never get back!" Over the roar of the storm, the brave captain called back, "We don't have to come back, but we must go out."

Not only did Nehemiah endure trouble from Israel's enemies, but he also dealt with struggles among the people of Israel themselves. Nehemiah 5 records a great controversy: as the work continued, the poorest workers were forced to mortgage their homes and fields to their brothers in order to survive; when they ran out of material things to sell, they had to sell their children into slavery—to their own brothers! It is not hard to imagine the desperation of these parents, who exclaimed, "We are forcing our sons and our daughters to be slaves, and some of our daughters have already been enslaved, but it is not in our power to help it, for other men have our fields and our vineyards" (Nehemiah 5:5).

Internal problems among God's people have an even greater potential of stopping a great work of God than external problems do. External threats tend to unite God's workers, while internal complications can easily divide the church. Great leaders understand the necessity of facing internal conflict quickly and impartially.

The details of how Nehemiah addressed the threat of internal strife are instructive:

> I was very angry when I heard their outcry and these words. I took counsel with myself, and I brought charges against the nobles and the officials. I said to them, "You are exacting interest, each from his

> brother." And I held a great assembly against them and said to them, "We, as far as we are able, have bought back our Jewish brothers who have been sold to the nations, but you even sell your brothers that they may be sold to us!" They were silent and could not find a word to say. So I said, "The thing that you are doing is not good. Ought you not to walk in the fear of our God to prevent the taunts of the nations our enemies? Moreover, I and my brothers and my servants are lending them money and grain. Let us abandon this exacting of interest. Return to them this very day their fields, their vineyards, their olive orchards, and their houses, and the percentage of money, grain, wine, and oil that you have been exacting from them." Then they said, "We will restore these and require nothing from them. We will do as you say." And I called the priests and made them swear to do as they had promised. I also shook out the fold of my garment and said, "So may God shake out every man from his house and from his labor who does not keep this promise. So may he be shaken out and emptied." And all the assembly said "Amen" and praised the Lord. And the people did as they had promised. (Nehemiah 5:6–13)

Take notice of how Nehemiah managed this crisis among the people and endured the storm. First, he *faced the crisis head-on* and expressed his anger. Nehemiah got the facts and assessed the degree of injustice taking place among the Jews before he voiced his frustration. Inspirational leaders understand that facts are friends. Moving forward on unsubstantiated impressions or feelings is unwise.

Second, Nehemiah *confronted the instigators of the problem directly* and personally with their shameful behavior. He didn't spread rumors or talk about their misdeeds behind their backs; instead he called an emergency meeting with those who had taken advantage of their brothers. When an internal crisis hits, great leaders do not allow themselves to become unfairly influenced by those who are rich or powerful in the church. Inspirational leaders make their decisions on the basis of God's Word and not according to political considerations.

Third, to correct the problem Nehemiah *used principles of conflict resolution*. Nehemiah honestly faced the rich with their injustices toward the poor and got them to agree to return all that they had taken from their less-privileged brothers. He went directly to the rich, before whom he laid out the problem, presented a solution, and negotiated a deal, and then he made them promise to fulfill their contract. This is an example of great leadership in action!

What happened next sets Nehemiah apart as an inspirational leader. In a stunning move, Nehemiah pledged to donate to the poorer Jews the money that the king had given him and his servants for their own yearly food allowance. Then he initiated a series of new policies: in a magnanimous gesture he ended the burdensome taxation policies of his predecessors, outlawed taking advantage of the poor, vowed not to purchase land, and sacrificed his personal wealth to feed every official, nobleman, and servant in his household (see Nehemiah 5:14–19).

Nehemiah's new policies were far more than a few remedies for injustice. As an inspirational leader, Nehemiah made the entire process a personal matter. His motivation is given in Nehemiah 5:15: "because of the fear of God." Nehemiah was a great inspirational leader because his first priority was God, and next to it was his commitment to the work of God: "I also persevered in the work on this wall" (Nehemiah 5:16).

Pastors must lead by example in their devotion to God, their commitment to the work of God, their love of the people of God, and their personal sacrifice. All great leaders must rest in God's timing when external or internal struggles threaten God's vision. They work through the problems with skill, equity, and love. The writer of Hebrews echoes this same principle in the life of Moses: "By faith [Moses] left Egypt, not being afraid of the anger of the king: for *he endured* as seeing him who is invisible" (Hebrews 11:27).

Think It Over: Ruling Wisely in Times of Crisis—Endurance

1. How do you handle delays in the vision God has given you? Do you wisely endure, or do you become anxious, frustrated, or impatient?
2. How do you handle difficult people, whether they are enemies of God or people within the church?
3. How prepared are you to boldly and biblically confront those who are stirring up conflict among the people you serve?
4. What will you do to personally sacrifice for the success of the vision God has given you?

Expect God to Do Great Things—Faith

Great leaders must trust God through the tests and trials that come with fulfilling His vision. As a result of this kind of faith, inspirational leaders will have reason to expect God to do great things. God always rewards faith that endures: "The wall was finished on the twenty-fifth day of the month Elul, in fifty-two days. And when all our enemies heard of it, all the nations around us were afraid and fell greatly in their own esteem, for they perceived that this work had been accomplished with the help of our God" (Nehemiah 6:15–16).

The completion of Jerusalem's gates and walls in only fifty-two days was more than remarkable—it was miraculous! Considering the complete destruction of the city by Nebuchadnezzar in 586 BC, the job of rebuilding the ramparts, gates, and walls in less than two months amid opposition was clearly a work of God through an inspirational leader and his devoted workers. The wall was so well rebuilt that parts of it are still standing today.

Nehemiah's faith was rewarded in other ways well beyond the physical reconstruction of the walls. The Bible tells us that Israel's enemies were frightened and defeated without the Jews firing an arrow because they perceived that the Lord had given Nehemiah divine assistance. Great spiritual leaders know that Satan is always trying to discourage, intimidate, and defeat believers: "Your adversary the devil prowls around like a roaring lion, seeking someone to devour" (1 Peter 5:8). In the middle of fulfilling God's work, Satan takes aim at the church, tempting God's people to give up or to give in to doubt or fear. He uses adverse circumstances from the outside or disruption on the inside. Satan's goal is to stop the work of God. Discouragement, external threats, and internal divisions are his strategies. But Satan is a defeated foe because of what Christ did on the cross for us: "The reason the Son of God appeared was to destroy the works of the devil" (1 John 3:8). God gets the last word every time.

That is what is so wonderful about Nehemiah's story—it has a surprise ending. When the work was completed and the wall dedicated, a spiritual revival broke out! The wall was appropriately finished on the Feast of Booths, or the Feast of Tabernacles—the Jewish holy day commemorating God's presence with Israel during their wanderings in the wilderness (see Leviticus 23:33–36). This feast day was perfectly timed for Nehemiah and the workers. On that day of dedication, Ezra read the Scriptures, and the people stood for hours to hear what they had not heard for a generation. Hearing the Word of God brought them under such deep conviction that they began to weep over their sins. Finally Ezra had to quiet their weeping and remind them that God's grace and power had returned to Jerusalem in full measure: "Do not be grieved, for the joy of the Lord is your strength" (Nehemiah 8:10). This powerful spiritual renewal was the eternal purpose that God had planned from the beginning—long before the rebuilding of the holy city had started. The vision that God had given Nehemiah and the workers was eternally greater than a rebuilt city—God's purpose was to rebuild the broken lives of His people!

The inspired spiritual leader never loses sight of the ultimate goal that God has for His people. God desires the church to grow spiritually, "until we all attain to the unity of the faith and of the knowledge of the Son of God, to mature manhood, to the measure of the stature of the fullness of Christ" (Ephesians 4:13).

Think It Over: Expect God to Do Great Things—Faith

1. What miracles are you seeing as the vision that God gave you is being fulfilled?
2. What changes in people's spiritual lives has the vision produced?
3. What unexpected things is God doing as the vision unfolds?
4. How will you give God the glory for what He has done?

CONCLUSION:
The Pastoral Leader as an Inspiring Trailblazer

Nehemiah is a wonderful model of an inspired, trailblazing leader. What is an inspired leader? It is a leader who, first of all, *intercedes* to know God's will. He *never* allows doubt to dominate but instead disciplines himself to hold fast in the face of opposition. An inspired leader *sees* a better future, or a vision of what will be, and he *passionately* communicates that vision to the people he serves. He *includes* and collaborates with others in order to bring about the fulfillment of the vision. He *rules* wisely in times of crisis and endures the storms, whether the trials come from without or within the church. And an inspired leader is strong in faith, *expecting* God to do great things to accomplish His vision. May God's men be inspired leaders who rally God's people to the fulfillment of God's vision for the church of Jesus Christ.

5

The Pastoral Leader and Prayer

Objective: *To stimulate pastors to deepen their prayer ministry by instructing them on the priorities to be had in prayer as well as the power, healing, and protection that prayer affords.*

Prayer may be the most underused resource that spiritual leaders have at their command. Through prayer a Christian leader communes with God (see Philippians 4:4–7), worships God (see Ephesians 1:15–23), listens to God (see 1 Samuel 3:2–14), expresses dependence on God (see 2 Corinthians 1:9–11), acknowledges his need for God (see 1 Samuel 1:9–17), calls on God to intervene in his circumstances (see 2 Samuel 15:31), accesses God's power (see James 5:16–18), moves the heart of God (see Job 42:10), claims the promises of God (see Daniel 9:17–19), and understands the will of God (see Colossians 1:9). This is why Jesus repeatedly commanded His disciples to pray (see Matthew 5:44; 7:7–11; 26:41; Luke 18:1; John 16:23) and taught them how to pray (see Matthew 6:5–13; John 14:13–14).

Given the impressive priority of prayer in the Bible, it seems strange that most spiritual leaders find it difficult to pray and to make prayer a personal priority. It is much easier to preach about prayer or to agree that prayer is an indispensible priority than to set aside time to pray. If the time every pastor spends in prayer were published, it would be cause for embarrassment to most pastors.

It is hard to understand why prayer is such a struggle until one realizes that it was also hard for the disciples. They could not understand why Jesus would spend entire nights in prayer (see Luke 11:1). What was so important about prayer that Jesus would sacrifice sleep to pray? The disciples were used to seeing Jesus rise before dawn to have unbroken communion with the Father (see Mark 1:35). Peter, James, and John witnessed Jesus transfigured, but what is often lost in the story is what preceded that explosion of luminescent glory—that Jesus initially took Peter, James, and John to the mountain to pray (see Luke 9:28). The disciples' lack of interest in prayer is illustrated in the Garden of Gethsemane, when He asked His disciples to watch and pray but within a short time they fell asleep (see Matthew 26:40–41). Jesus highlighted their problem, which is one that every spiritual leader experiences: "The spirit indeed is willing, but the flesh is weak" (Matthew 26:41).

Mastering prayer is like anything else—it takes time and discipline. Keeping the priority and discipline of prayer is as central to the success of all ministry today as it was to the life of Jesus in the first century.

Three Kinds of Prayer

Jesus taught three basic types of prayer in the Sermon on the Mount: "*Ask*, and it will be given to you; *seek*, and you will find; *knock*, and it will be opened to you. For everyone who asks receives, and the one who seeks finds, and to the one who knocks it will be opened" (Matthew 7:7–8). Jesus placed each mode of prayer in the present tense, indicating that we should continue asking, seeking, and knocking.

The first type of prayer is *asking*, which is the simplest transaction between God and the praying disciple. We ask and keep on asking, and God answers and continues to answer. As He does, we receive and continue to receive from Him.

Asking is how most Christians practice prayer. They have an unmet need that is beyond their ability, so they are prompted to ask God to give them what they lack. Many times when they ask, they receive an immediate answer from God. This kind of prayer is the most basic of all transactions between God and the praying disciple. But in reality this first kind of prayer requires very little faith.

The second kind of prayer is *seeking*, and it is not as easy as the first, because Christians are sometimes unsure if the thing they are praying for is in God's will. This second dimension of prayer requires us to seek and keep on seeking.

In seeking kinds of prayers, we search ourselves, and we pursue God to know His will. Seeking prayers require us to refine and refocus our requests, because sometimes we pray with wrong motives (see James 4:3) or perhaps with hidden sins that keep God from answering us (see Psalm 66:18). Sometimes God is leading us to resolve broken relationships before He will answer us (see Matthew 5:24; 1 Peter 3:7), and at other times it is just a matter of waiting on the Lord for His timing (see Psalm 27:14).

The third dimension of prayer that Jesus described is *knocking*. Some prayers are like spiritual battering rams that remove barriers. At times the door to answered prayer is shut because of adverse circumstances, people who oppose us, or spiritual resistance. In these times of battle, we face opposition, and we feel locked out of God's throne room. This third dimension of prayer requires us to keep knocking in believing prayer until the door opens. Some battles are only won through knocking kinds of prayers that break down every stronghold and claim the victory.

Think It Over: Three Kinds of Prayer

1. Why do you think it is so hard for pastors and leaders to pray? If you knew that God would bless your church more if you prayed, would you pray more?
2. What are some of the simplest *asking* prayers that you are currently praying?
3. What *seeking* prayers are you praying that need God's refinement or guidance to help you know how to pray?
4. *Knocking* prayers require faith and perseverance. What prayers are you praying in which you sense resistance against you? Can you discern where the resistance is coming from? Is it satanic? Circumstantial? Human?

Priorities in Prayer

In the course of ministry, a pastor is presented regularly with a great many needs. How is he to pray for so many people and situations, not to mention his own and his family's needs? And while it is vital that a pastor lift his needs and the needs of his church to the Lord, God also desires believers to spend time in prayer praising Him, confessing sin to Him, and thanking Him. How can a pastor balance his prayer life to cover all these bases?

A helpful guide on how to balance our prayers comes from the acrostic A.C.T.S.: adoration, confession, thanksgiving, and supplication. A.C.T.S. provides an easy way to help leaders remember key elements of prayer.

Adoration—"Blessed be God!" (Psalm 68:35). Adoration prayers tell God how much we appreciate Him. In adoration we express our love for God, and we praise His power and majesty. This is a great way for a pastor to begin his prayer time. "How awesome are your deeds!" (Psalm 66:3).

Confession—"If we confess our sins, he is faithful and just to forgive us our sins and to cleanse us from all unrighteousness" (1 John 1:9). Confession prayer is agreeing with God in the areas in which we have sinned. When we confess our sins, we should be specific. Then we must claim the forgiveness that we have in Christ and ask for help and strength to turn away from future temptations.

Thanksgiving—We are to always "magnify him with thanksgiving" (Psalm 69:30). In thanksgiving prayers we thank God for His love, faithfulness, patience, and many other kindnesses toward us. In this kind of prayer we express gratitude for what God is doing in our life. We thank Jesus for dying on the cross for us. We thank the Holy Spirit for indwelling us and never leaving us.

Supplication—"Let your requests be made known to God" (Philippians 4:6). Supplication prayers tell God what we need and what others need. When we pray this way, we believe God for the answers to our prayers, no matter how small or impossible they seem to us. Supplication requests are never too big or too small to God our Creator and Redeemer. In supplication we pray for the needs of others by interceding for them in prayer. In other words, we carry someone's burdens to God.

When it comes to supplication, what specific kinds of requests should a leader have? Below are some biblical priorities that a pastor should include in his prayer life:

- Pray for faith, and pray in faith (see Mark 11:24).
- Pray to abide in Christ with God's Word abiding in you (see John 15:7).
- Pray for your needs and the specific needs of others (see 2 Corinthians 12:8; 1 Thessalonians 5:25; Hebrews 13:18).
- Pray for the spread of the gospel (see Colossians 4:3; 2 Thessalonians 3:1).
- Pray to confess your sins (see 1 John 1:9).
- Pray for deliverance from Satan and the influences of evil men (see Luke 22:31–32; 2 Thessalonians 3:1–2).
- Pray for resistance in temptation (see Matthew 26:41).
- Pray for strength and encouragement to endure (see Ephesians 3:14–16).
- Pray for the fullness of Christ's character to be seen in your life (see Ephesians 3:17).
- Pray for wisdom and spiritual insight (see Ephesians 3:18–19; James 1:5–6).
- Pray for an understanding of God's will (see Colossians 1:9).
- Pray for a closer relationship with God (see Ephesians 1:17).
- Pray for physical and spiritual healing (see James 5:13–16).
- Pray specifically for people who you know are without Christ (see Romans 10:1; 1 Timothy 2:1).
- Pray for political rulers and authorities (see 1 Timothy 2:1–2).
- Pray for the peace of Christ to rule in your heart (see Philippians 4:6–7).
- Pray for the needs of all the saints (see Ephesians 6:18).
- Pray for the persecuted church (see Ephesians 6:20).

A practical tool that can help a pastor keep his prayer priorities balanced is a prayer journal. Writing down praises, confessions, thanksgivings, and requests and then recording the answers to prayer that God gives can be encouraging and faith-inspiring. It also produces a record of testimonies that can be shared with a pastor's congregation and used to help the flock grow in prayer as well.

Another helpful discipline for spiritual leaders can be to write out the full text of their prayers. Paul, for example, wrote his prayers into his letters as encouragement and instruction for the early churches (see Ephesians 1:15–19; Colossians 1:9–12).

Think It Over: Priorities in Prayer

1. What do the four letters of A.C.T.S. stand for? Considering the A.C.T.S. method, how balanced is your prayer life?
2. What are your current prayer priorities regarding your life? Your family? Your ministry?
3. What promise of God's Word can you claim regarding these requests?
4. Do you keep a prayer journal? If not, challenge yourself to try it for a week, and see if it doesn't become a long-term habit.

Prayer and Spiritual Warfare

Prayer is a lethal spiritual weapon in the battle against Satan: "We do not wrestle against flesh and blood, but against the rulers, against the authorities, against the cosmic powers over this present darkness, against the spiritual forces of evil in the heavenly places . . . praying at all times in the Spirit, with all prayer and supplication" (Ephesians 6:12,18).

Every disciple is commanded to oppose Satan in prayer. The praying believer wields no personal power or human authority capable of withstanding the onslaught of Satan, but every follower of Jesus stands in the delegated and final authority of the risen and victorious Christ who has "all authority in heaven and on earth" (Matthew 28:18). Jesus came "to destroy the works of the devil" (1 John 3:8). Praying in confidence against spiritual resistance is done in Jesus' name and in His authority. This assertive power is our God-given right, purchased by the finished work of Christ.

In Matthew 12:29 Jesus likened Satan to a strong man who is fully armed and dangerous. Jesus said that the only way to enter Satan's territory and claim victory is to first bind the enemy. What could this mean except that Satan can be bound and his evil work neutralized by the authority of Jesus? Prayer is how the spiritual leader goes on the attack against Satan, binds him, and plunders his evil kingdom. This vital lesson in spiritual warfare cannot be overstated. The spiritual leader who attempts to go up against Satan in spiritual war must use the lethal weapon of prayer, or he will be overtaken and defeated.

Think It Over: Prayer and Spiritual Warfare

1. By whose authority does a pastor wage war against Satan? Why is it important to understand this?
2. How does prayer figure into the spiritual battle that every pastor faces?
3. To what temptations are you most vulnerable?
4. What specific defenses does God's Word give you to claim victory over temptation?

Prayer for the Sick

One need that a pastoral leader is often faced with is the need for healing. While believers have many perspectives on this issue, James 5:14–16 gives us specific instruction on the matter of prayer and anointing for healing:

> Is anyone among you sick? Let him call for the elders of the church, and let them pray over him, anointing him with oil in the name of the Lord. And the prayer of faith will save the one who is sick, and the Lord will raise him up. And if he has committed sins, he will be forgiven. Therefore, confess your sins to one another and pray for one another, that you may be healed. The prayer of a righteous man has great power as it is working.

Before we consider what this passage tells us about healing, let's look first at two things that this passage does *not* say.

First, this passage *does not reject or belittle the use of doctors and modern medicine*. It is not a sin to seek the advice and care of a medical doctor. Jesus Himself, the greatest of all healers, said in Matthew 9:12, "Those who are well have no need of a physician, but those who are sick." God chose Luke, the beloved physician, to record the life of Christ in careful detail from the birth of Christ to the development of the church in Acts. The apostle Paul, who in Jesus' name performed many miracles of healing to authenticate the message of the gospel to the Gentiles, prescribed for Timothy, "No longer drink only water, but use a little wine for the sake of your stomach and your frequent ailments" (1 Timothy 5:23). If anyone claiming to represent Christ says that we should avoid medical treatment because it shows a lack of faith, don't believe them. That is false teaching.

Second, this passage *does not say that everyone who gets sick is guaranteed a miraculous healing*. Some preachers have erroneously taught that it is God's will that everyone be healed. Those who promote these teachings make it sound as if we have a right to *demand* healing from God and that God *must* comply. The Bible does not teach that believers have the right to demand anything they want from God.

The Bible teaches that at times, for God's higher purposes, He allows certain Christians to suffer illness for His glory. On one of his missionary journeys, the apostle Paul left one of his traveling missionaries, Trophimus, sick at Miletus (see 2 Timothy 4:20). Paul also tells us in 2 Corinthians 12:7–8 that he asked God three times to remove his own "thorn in the flesh" (NASB), but the illness was not removed. Instead God told him, "My grace is sufficient for you, for my power is made perfect in weakness" (2 Corinthians 12:9). Paul did not complain and protest because God had not healed him. He did not feel disappointed with God or continuously demand that God change his situation. Here is how Paul handled his chronic illness: "For the sake of Christ, then, I am content with weaknesses, insults, hardships, persecutions, and calamities. For when I am weak, then I am strong" (2 Corinthians 12:10). In this experience of Paul, the power of God was not seen in a healing but in the daily grace to carry on.

Sometimes God answers our prayers for healing by saying, "I am going to let the affliction stay, but I am going to use it to demonstrate My power by giving you My overwhelming grace to live with it." Never forget that sometimes it is God's will that sickness remain so that His grace might be poured out to compensate for human weakness. Grace to endure suffering is as great a gift from God as a miracle of healing.

So what is the pattern of biblical prayer for healing? What steps can a spiritual leader take to comply with the Word of God for those who are sick? Let's look at seven steps regarding healing that James 5 lays out for us.

First, *the sick person begins the process for healing.* "Is anyone among you sick? Let him call for the elders of the church, and let them pray over him" (James 5:14). The process of healing prayer is begun by the sick Christian. In essence, this is the act of faith and obedience required of the sick. When a sick believer calls the leaders of the church to pray for him, that person is saying, "I believe that the elders ought to seek God for my healing." By that simple act a sick Christian says, "I believe that God *can* heal me and that He should be asked for that miracle."

This first step is important, because it requires the sick to *desire* healing. When Jesus passed the pool of Bethesda, one man lying beside the pool had been sick for thirty-eight years. John 5:6 tells us what happened: "When Jesus saw him lying there and knew that he had already been there a long time, he said to him, 'Do you want to be healed?'" God does not do something *to* us that we do not want done *for* us.

Second, *the elders of the church are to be called for prayer.* "Let him call for the elders of the church, and let them pray over him" (James 5:14). Prayer for healing is *not* a solo effort by the pastor but a joint effort by the church leadership. Spiritual leaders are charged with the task of praying for the sick.

Spiritual leadership should always cover the church with prayer. The prophet Samuel exclaimed, "Far be it from me that I should sin against the Lord by ceasing to pray for you" (1 Samuel 12:23). Paul taught Timothy, "I urge that supplications, prayers, intercessions, and thanksgivings be made for all people" (1 Timothy 2:1). Ministry success rises and falls on the prayer life of the leaders.

God is looking for leaders who are totally dependent on Him. In healing prayer leaders put the sick before God and call on His healing power. Elders are not perfect men, but they must be men who seek to do things God's way. James uses Elijah as the example: "Elijah was a man with a nature like ours, and he prayed fervently that it might not rain, and for three years and six months it did not rain on the earth. Then he prayed again, and heaven gave rain, and the earth bore its fruit" (James 5:17–18). Why does God choose to use *righteous* men and not simply men who just have a position in the church? Because purity in life is the key to powerful praying. When a leader's life is pure, he has faith to ask God for what seems impossible.

Third, *the sick are commanded to confess their sins.* "Confess your sins to one another and pray for one another, that you may be healed" (James 5:16). Why is the issue of sin raised at a prayer meeting for healing?

Sin and healing are related for two reasons. The first reason is that *some* illnesses are a result of persistent sin and a lack of repentance. Throughout the Bible, sickness in some people's lives can be traced right back to their weak spiritual lives. In Numbers 12:1–15 we read that Miriam were struck with leprosy for seven days because she and Aaron had rebelled against Moses, God's appointed leader. Numbers 21:4–9 reads that Israel grumbled against God in the wilderness, and God sent fiery serpents that bit the people and made them sick. And 1 Corinthians 11:27–30 tells us how some Christians became sick because they partook of the Lord's table in an unworthy manner. Persistent and unforgiven sins are serious business! Sins can make us sick.

The second reason that confession of sin and healing are related is because, simply stated, sin blocks prayer from being heard: "If I had cherished iniquity in my heart, the Lord would not have listened" (Psalm 66:18). When the sick confess their sins, they pave the way for God to hear the prayer for healing. The elders' sins as well can dull their prayers, so every elder must examine his spiritual condition before offering up prayer for the sick. That is why James says, "Confess your sins to *one another.*" Elders are to be righteous men who pray for areas of spiritual weakness as well as physical healing. Sin is a deeper sickness than anything physical. Biblical healing involves the whole person—body, mind, and spirit.

Fourth, *the sick are anointed with oil.* "Let them pray over him, anointing him with oil" (James 5:14). The oil used in healing prayer is not medicinal but a symbol of the anointing of God (see Exodus 28:41; 29:7,29; 1 Samuel 16:3). Anointing with oil was a common practice in the Old Testament for priests, prophets, and kings. This anointing was not to heal them but an outward sign of the blessing of God that had come upon them. It was a consecration for service.

For instance, when Samuel anointed David as king of Israel, the Spirit of the Lord came upon David to bless him. While James does not clearly state the purpose of the oil, it seems clear from the rest of Scripture that the oil symbolizes the coming of the Holy Spirit upon a person for a specific work. The sick person who is anointed and prayed for should understand that whatever the outcome of the elders' prayer—whether God should heal him or give him grace to bear the illness—he is being consecrated for whatever future service that God should require of him. The idea of getting healed so that the sick person can return to a normal life independent of doing God's will is unbiblical. Anointing is for blessing and service.

Fifth, *the sick are anointed in the name of the Lord.* "Let them pray over him, anointing him with oil in the name of the Lord" (James 5:14). The powerful name of Jesus is to be used in praying for the sick. Whatever happens as a result of the elders' prayers, Jesus receives the glory and credit.

Jesus commanded His disciples to pray in His name: "Whatever you ask in my name, this I will do" (John 14:13). Peter and John discovered the power of Jesus' name when they said to the lame man by the beautiful gate in Jerusalem, "In the name of Jesus Christ of Nazareth, rise up and walk!" (Acts 3:6). Later Peter told the watching crowd in Acts 3:16, "His [Jesus'] name—by faith in his name—has made this man strong whom you see and know, and the faith that is through Jesus has given the man this perfect health." The name of Jesus is the most powerful name in the universe. After His resurrection Jesus told His disciples, "All authority in heaven and on earth has been given to me" (Matthew 28:18).

Sixth, *the elders are to pray in faith.* "The prayer of faith will save the one who is sick" (James 5:15). Elders should not pray in a timid or apprehensive manner. Elders are called to pray with expectation for restoration and healing: "This is the confidence that we have toward [God], that if we ask anything according to his will he hears us. And if we know that he hears us in whatever we ask, we know that we have the requests that we have asked of him" (1 John 5:14–15). The elders' prayer for the sick is to be "the prayer of faith." Faith is the active ingredient that considers our request to be an accomplished fact. God gives us a special kind of confidence for this kind of praying. Prayer for the sick must be expectant; the elders must be poised to see God perform a miracle. However, this is not demanding or manipulative prayer. It is simply trusting in God to do what is best.

And seventh, *the Lord does the healing according to His will.* "The Lord will raise him up" (James 5:15). In this phrase we can clearly see the sovereignty of God. God may choose to answer the prayer for healing in one of three ways:

- God may instantly heal the sick *without* the aid of doctors or medicine. "In the name of Jesus Christ of Nazareth, rise up and walk" (Acts 3:6).
- God may progressively heal the sick either with or without the aid of doctors or medicine. Luke 17:14 says, "As they went they were cleansed."
- God may give the sick person a miraculous measure of grace to endure the illness. "My grace is sufficient for you, for my power is made perfect in weakness" (2 Corinthians 12:9).

Prayer for healing is one of the spiritual responsibilities and rights of an elder, including the pastor. Few activities a spiritual leader is asked to perform call for this level of humility and faith. Therefore, it is to be undertaken within scriptural guidelines and with great anticipation of the amazing things that God will do as a result of our prayers.

Think It Over: Prayer for the Sick

1. What are the seven steps that James 5 gives for praying for someone's healing?
2. What is the responsibility of the sick person? What is the responsibility of the elders?
3. What are the three ways in which God answers prayers for healing?
4. When physical healing does not come, how do we know that God has not failed us?

Prayer and Fasting

Fasting is voluntarily abstaining from food for the purpose of humbling ourselves before God in prayer. The spiritual discipline of fasting usually does not mean abstaining from water. Jesus began His public ministry with a forty-day fast, and Matthew 4:2 says that after forty days "he was hungry." If Jesus had gone without water, the Bible would have recorded that He became thirsty, since thirst precedes hunger. (A caution regarding fasting: people with preexisting medical conditions must be careful when fasting not to endanger their health or abuse their bodies.)

The primary purpose of fasting is to voluntarily humble oneself before the Lord. This act of self-denial takes the emphasis off the needs of the body and allows God to lift us up to new levels of godly living. God places this responsibility of humbling ourselves on us. Many Scriptures resonate with this theme:

> Whoever humbles himself like this child is the greatest in the kingdom of heaven. (Matthew 18:4)

> Whoever exalts himself will be humbled, and whoever humbles himself will be exalted. (Matthew 23:12)

> Humble yourselves before the Lord, and he will exalt you. (James 4:10)

> Humble yourselves, therefore, under the mighty hand of God so that at the proper time he may exalt you. (1 Peter 5:6)

> I humbled my soul with fasting. (Psalm 35:13, NASB)

What are some of the purposes of fasting? We find many reasons for fasting in the Bible, both in the Old Testament and the New Testament:

- Physical protection from an enemy (see Ezra 8:21–23)
- Power and wisdom during a stressful circumstance (see 2 Chronicles 20:1–12)
- To have times of personal cleansing from sin (see Leviticus 16:29–31)
- Before inaugurating a new ministry challenge (see Luke 3:21–22; 4:1–2)
- When victory was needed over satanic temptations (see Matthew 4:1–11)
- When seeking God's will about spiritual leadership (see Acts 13:1–4)
- As part of the total life of a dedicated servant of Jesus Christ (see 2 Corinthians 6:4–6)

No matter our reason for fasting, fasting is intended to change us. A constant battle goes on inside every Christian between the Spirit and our old sinful nature. The Bible tells us, "The desires of the flesh are against the Spirit, and the desires of the Spirit are against the flesh, for these are opposed to each other, to keep you from doing the things you want to do" (Galatians 5:17). Old sinful ways of thinking and sinful attitudes, however, undermine the wonderful things God desires to do in our lives. The center of the action is our thought life: "The mind that is set on the flesh is hostile to God, for it does not submit to God's law; indeed, it cannot. Those who are in the flesh cannot please God" (Romans 8:7–8). The internal war is won when the Christian denies himself and surrenders to the indwelling Holy Spirit: "Walk by the Spirit, and you will not gratify the desires of the flesh" (Galatians 5:16).

Paul said, "I discipline my body and keep it under control, lest after preaching to others I myself should be disqualified" (1 Corinthians 9:27). Fasting serves notice to our bodies and to our sinful nature that they are not our master. The body is a wonderful servant but a terrible master. Fasting enables the Christian to run his race like a well-trained athlete.

Jesus warned His disciples not to make a public display of fasting in an effort to impress others. Instead we are to look well groomed and ready to meet the day: "When you fast, anoint your head and wash your face, that your fasting may not be seen by others but by your Father who is in secret. And your Father who sees in secret will reward you" (Matthew 6:17–18).

There is simply no way to fully measure the impact of fasting this side of heaven. Examples of the results of fasting in Scripture are nothing short of amazing:

- The entire wicked city of Nineveh repented en masse and turned to God (see Jonah 3:1–6). Fasting laid the groundwork for a great spiritual awakening.
- Citywide violence and evil ways came to an end (see Jonah 3:10). Fasting brought an end to the kinds of social problems that defile and destroy cities.
- A Persian king made a decree to spare the Jewish nation (see Esther 4:15–17; 5:1–3; 7:3–6; 8:3–8). Fasting kept an evil government from a disastrous policy.

Some Christians are not sure whether fasting is for today or not, but Jesus answered this question for us when He was gathered with a large group at the home of Matthew. The Pharisees disapproved of the party going on at Matthew's home because Jesus was with tax collectors and sinners. They whined, "The disciples of John fast often and offer prayers, and so do the disciples of the Pharisees, but yours eat and drink" (Luke 5:33). The Pharisee meant this to be a criticism of Jesus.

How Jesus answered them is a message for us today and answers the question of whether fasting is for the Christian today: "Can you make wedding guests fast while the bridegroom is with them? The days will come when the bridegroom is taken away from them, and then they will fast in those days" (Luke 5:34–35). Jesus taught that fasting is for the time between His ascension to heaven and His glorious return to Earth. Until Jesus comes again, fasting is not only desirable for us but necessary.

Think It Over: Prayer and Fasting

1. What is the purpose of fasting?
2. When is fasting a good prayer decision? When is it not a good decision?
3. If you were to fast and pray, what major miracle would you ask God for?

A Pastor's Personal Prayer Team

One thing that can easily be overlooked by a busy pastor is his need to have others praying for him, his family, and his ministry. For a pastor to be effective in ministry, he needs to develop a team of people who will pray specifically for these things.

Some years ago I was asked to be on the leadership team for the Billy Graham Crusade. The night before the crusade, the leadership team had a meeting with Dr. Graham. I had never personally met Billy Graham, but knowing that he was the world's greatest living evangelist, I came wanting to learn from this great man of God. I will never forget what I heard. He said to those of us gathered that day, "Many of you think that because I have come to your city, God will do great things here, but I am here to tell you that God will do nothing great apart from *your* prayers. So pray, pray, pray!" Billy Graham knew that every great man of God and every great move of God through that man is the product of prayer by a team of dedicated believers standing behind him.

Church historians attest to this fact as well. C. H. Spurgeon said, "Whenever God determines to do a great work, He first sets His people to pray." Spurgeon had discovered that neither his sermons nor his good works were responsible for the spiritual impact of his ministry; rather, it was his prayer team that moved the hand of God.

This is not a new concept. It goes all the way back to the Old Testament, to the book of Exodus, when Moses helped Joshua defeat the Amalekites by sitting on a hilltop and holding the staff of God above his head in a posture of prayer. Aaron and Hur held up Moses' weary arms, and with their help victory was secured (see Exodus 17:10–11). This concept is also found in the New Testament, when 120 disciples prayed in the days following Jesus' ascension. On the Day of Pentecost, when the Holy Spirit arrived, the prayers of the 120 resulted in the bold preaching of a previously sin-broken fisherman named Peter, and three thousand people were converted (see Acts 1:12–14; 2:1–41).

We find a number of reasons in Scripture why a pastor must have a prayer team that prays especially for him, his family, and his ministry. Here are seven:

- Prayer for spiritual leaders by the church is God's will (see 1 Thessalonians 5:25).
- Prayer is the only way that pastors can successfully fulfill their accountability to God (see James 3:1).
- Prayer empowers preaching (see Ephesians 6:19–20).
- Prayer is the best defense against Satan's attacks (see Ephesians 6:18; 1 Peter 5:8).
- Prayer protects a pastor from being vulnerable to temptation (see Luke 22:31–32).
- Prayer is essential because of a pastor's visibility and influence (see 1 Samuel 12:13–14).
- Prayer is crucial for the effectiveness of the pastor's ministry (see Colossians 4:3–4).

I wish I had learned this powerful secret in my first years of ministry, but I now know the value and impact of a personal prayer team. Each week I meet with a small group of men who are my personal prayer warriors. I share with them details about my life, my family, and my ministry needs with full confidence that they will pray over these matters. I also require every pastor and minister on my staff to meet weekly with their own personal prayer teams. One day when I get to heaven, I will learn of all the miracles that God did because of my prayer team, and I will also learn of how Satan's schemes against me, my family, and my ministry were thwarted because of these men's prayers. To God be the glory!

Think It Over: A Pastor's Personal Prayer Team

1. If you were to start a prayer team for you and your family, which men would you choose?
2. What time would be best for this group of men to meet?
3. When will you begin?

CONCLUSION:
The Pastoral Leader and Prayer

Spiritual leaders who take prayer seriously make decisions about praying. They schedule prayer into their day, and they keep a prayer journal of the requests they make before God and the answers they receive. Faithfully practicing these two simple disciplines will revolutionize a pastor's prayer life.

6

The Pastoral Leader and Preaching

***Objective:** To provide an in-depth step-by-step process to help the pastor maximize his skill and spiritual impact in preaching.*

Preaching is God's ordained method for communicating the gospel to the world and for equipping the saints for ministry. Without preaching the world would never know the truth about God, and the church would not be prepared for ministry:

> Since, in the wisdom of God, the world did not know God through wisdom, it pleased God through the folly of what we preach to save those who believe (1 Corinthians 1:21).

> He gave the apostles, the prophets, the evangelists, the shepherds and teachers, to equip the saints for the work of ministry, for building up the body of Christ (Ephesians 4:11–12).

Since God established such high purposes for preaching, every pastor should desire to improve his effectiveness as a preacher.

In a moment of sheer honesty, my wife once said to me, "It should be a crime to bore people with the Word of God." Since hearing that comment I've worked hard never to fall into that trap. The Word of God is "living and active, sharper than any two-edged sword, piercing to the division of soul and of spirit" (Hebrews 4:12), and giving a congregation dull and wearisome preaching is one crime that no pastor should ever commit.

I have a simple definition for preaching: it is boldly communicating the truth of God from the Word of God with the heart of God in the power of the Spirit of God through the man of God to the people of God and to the lost world that God loves. Preaching is not merely the art of making a sermon and delivering it; preaching is God's sacred work of making a preacher into a man of God and delivering a message through that man's life! In biblical preaching the message cannot be separated from the messenger. This puts the preacher in a responsible and holy place.

The New Testament uses three Greek words to describe preaching:

1. *Euangelizo*, "to speak good tidings" (see Mark 3:14; 16:15). This word is mostly used in connection with communicating God's offer of forgiveness and eternal life through the finished work of Christ. All good preaching includes the good news of Jesus Christ.
2. *Kerugma*, "a royal proclamation by a herald" (see Romans 10:14–15; 2 Corinthians 5:20). This indicates the prophetic nature of the preacher. A preacher speaks for God, the sovereign King of the universe. His authoritative message is designed to compel a decision.
3. *Parrhesiazomai*, "to be bold in speech" (see Acts 9:26–27). Effective preaching requires moral and spiritual boldness. It has been said that preaching should comfort the afflicted but afflict the comfortable.

Good preaching will include all three of these facets: it will proclaim the good news of the gospel, contain the authority of God the King, and be bold and unafraid in confronting moral issues.

New Testament preaching is fundamentally designed to fulfill God's purposes rather than to attract an audience or express the preacher's preferences. Wherever preaching is mentioned in the New Testament, six basic intentions drive it:

- To reveal Jesus (see Acts 5:42; 8:35; 10:36; 11:20; 17:18; 1 Corinthians 1:23; 2 Corinthians 4:5)
- To present the gospel to unbelievers (see Romans 10:14; 1 Corinthians 1:21; Colossians 4:3–4)
- To grow Christians in the grace and knowledge of God (see Acts 14:7–9; Romans 10:8; 2 Peter 3:18)

- To equip believers to serve (see Ephesians 4:11–12)
- To demonstrate the power of God (see Mark 3:14–15; 16:20; 1 Corinthians 2:4)
- To warn people of false teaching and to teach sound doctrine (see Colossians 1:28; 2 Timothy 4:1–2; Titus 1:9; 2:1)

Not all preaching qualifies as biblical or effective in fulfilling God's purposes. Some types of preaching and preachers we should avoid. While some of these types of preaching may appear to be successful, they depart from God's main intention for this ministry.

The following are types of preaching to avoid:

- The *therapeutic pulpit*, from which the pastor brings psychology lessons
- The *human-potential motivational pulpit*, from which the object is to coach people on human potential and how to be a success
- The *prosperity pulpit*, from which the pastor's preaching is designed to enrich himself and persuade people to chase after the false hope of wealth
- The *opinion pulpit*, from which the pastor uses a verse of Scripture as a springboard to give his opinion on a wide range of issues
- The *political pulpit*, from which the governmental agenda of a political party is top priority
- The *preach-me pulpit*, from which the pastor manipulates the message to be about him
- The *feel-good pulpit*, from which the goal is to tell people what they want to hear in order to make everyone happy
- The *angry pulpit*, from which the pastor's tone is judgmental and from which he always seems to be on the attack against someone or something

To be an effective and biblical preacher, a pastor can apply several principles to his ministry. We will spend this chapter exploring *seven steps* for godly preaching: preparation, dedication, interpretation, organization, proclamation, application, and preservation. These steps are connected to each other like a fine string of pearls—the beauty of one step enhances that of the next. Exploring these steps will enable a pastor to understand

God's plan for the sacred task of preaching and the responsibilities of the preacher.

Preparation of the Preacher for Preaching

The first step to effective preaching is careful preparation: "Do your best to present yourself to God as one approved, a worker who has no need to be ashamed, rightly handling the word of truth" (2 Timothy 2:15).

In the pioneer days of the American Wild West, a man who went to a gunfight unprepared was said to "shoot from the hip," meaning that he hadn't taken time to aim. This could be said of some preachers and their preaching. They go unprepared into the spiritual battleground of the pulpit and "shoot from the lip," never aiming their message. The tragedy of this is that while the Wild West gunfighter will end up physically dead, the preacher is spiritually dead.

To carefully prepare to preach, a pastor must first and foremost *set aside time* for this task. The busyness of pastoral ministry can easily consume a pastor's schedule until no time is left for the top priority of preaching. Some pastors neglect preaching preparation because they like the feeling of being needed by individuals in their church. But after a busy week of ministry, these deeply compassionate pastors go into the pulpit emotionally drained and with limited preparation. Good preachers learn to say no to *good* things so that the *best* things can get done. Setting aside regular sermon preparation time must be a priority in order for a pastor to become an effective preacher. At least one day a week is a good goal.

Prepared preachers also know the value of *being curious and knowledgeable about a wide range of subjects*. The education level of the average church member has risen. This means that a pastor must be accurate in his facts and well informed on topics. To advance in effectiveness, every preacher should be a self-starter and a perpetual learner. He should make a practice of reading materials other than pastoral books and journals, attending seminars that raise the level of his understanding of the Bible and the world around him, and pursuing formal education if he can. But no matter how he approaches it, he should never stop learning. Knowledge about philosophy, art, history, education, psychology, and science will enrich a pastor's understanding of the world that God created and help him connect his flock's faith to their lives outside the church.

Good preachers stay current with local news and world events. Pastors who discern the world around them can be a prophetic or comforting voice in the face of a community tragedy or an international disaster and can also bring a biblical perspective to moral issues that are the subject of a national or cultural debate.

In 2015 the United States Supreme Court ruled that gay marriage was legal in all fifty states. This matter riveted the attention of everyone in America; the moral and biblical implications of the court's decision was on every Christian's mind. When the ruling was handed down, it shocked the nation. My flock was wounded and wondering how to view this attack on the natural family and on biblical morality, so the next weekend I responded with a biblical approach to the news.

I voiced my regret that five of the nine justices had made a sweeping decision to legalize gay marriage. I proclaimed that this law was against God's Word and did not conform to a Christian worldview. I pointed out the historical significance of this decision by saying that the five judges had arrogantly ignored thousands of years of Western civilization. I quoted from the legal opinion of one of the dissenting judges, who warned of the danger to democracy that this decision posed. I reminded the people that America had been built on the freedom of religion and the right of conscience.

Then I assumed the preacher's prophetic role and clearly proclaimed that this was one of those times when God calls His people to obey Him rather than men because this ruling violated Scripture. Then I reminded my church that as the moral foundation of America shifts and breaks, American Christians will become part of the counterculture. I said that we should not fear but become even bolder in our witness, because this is the pattern found in Acts as well as in the countries of many of our Christian brothers and sisters around the world.

Then I appealed to them in my role as an evangelist by saying that the church needs to develop a new love for gay people. Homosexuals need Jesus, and the only way to reach them is with the love of God. Our Christian viewpoint is not about hating gays or any sinner. We are called to love everyone and to declare the gospel of Jesus Christ, which is the only message powerful enough to transform the human heart and give new life. God calls the preacher to be like the sons of Issachar, who were "men who had understanding of the times, to know what Israel ought to do" (1 Chronicles 12:32).

Good preparation also means that a preacher will *plan out his preaching schedule in advance*. The emotional tyranny of asking "What should I preach on this week?" is oppressive and unnecessary. Unless the Holy Spirit calls for a last-minute change, the effective preacher should not preach last-minute sermons that come from last-minute planning.

Another advantage in advance planning is that the preacher can excite the people about next week's message and motivate them to come and hear what God has to say. I highly recommend series preaching through a book of the Bible or on a biblical theme. Series preaching will accomplish two important goals: First, the preacher will know in advance where he is going so that he can pray for spiritual insight on the matter. Second, preaching through a book of the Bible will force the preacher to speak on subjects that are part of the whole counsel of God. Series preaching eliminates hobby preaching or camping on a pastor's favorite topic.

Think It Over: Preparation of the Preacher for Preaching

1. Describe your normal routine for preparation for preaching.
2. What could you do to prepare your sermons with greater ease and effectiveness?
3. What resources do you use to keep yourself updated on the latest international and local news?
4. What kind of preaching series suits you best? Book study? Topical preaching?
5. How does planning your preaching schedule in advance help you, your staff, and the people you serve?

Dedication of the Preacher for Preaching

The second step to powerful biblical preaching is dedication: "If anyone cleanses himself from what is dishonorable, he will be a vessel for honorable use, set apart as holy, useful to the master of the house, ready for every good work" (2 Timothy 2:21).

How does the preacher become an instrument of God for honorable use? A preacher must have the same attitude as a runner getting ready for a big race or a weightlifter getting his body primed for competition: every athlete knows that in order to win, he must totally dedicate himself to his task in advance of the event.

The apostle Paul spoke of his careful dedication to personal preparation:

> Do you not know that in a race all the runners run, but only one receives the prize? So run that you may obtain it. Every athlete exercises self-control in all things. They do it to receive a perishable wreath, but we an imperishable. So I do not run aimlessly; I do not box as one beating the air. But I discipline my body and keep it under control, lest after preaching to others I myself should be disqualified. (1 Corinthians 9:24–27)

Three *p*'s of personal dedication will help the preacher give his best: prayer, practice, and personal care.

Dedicating the Preacher's Spirit in Prayer

The preacher God uses must develop the seed thoughts and ideas for his message in prayer. The obvious question facing the preacher in preparing his message is "What does God want me to say? From which text, topic, or passage should I draw the message?" Without a prayerful conviction that God is providing the inspiration for a subject, the preacher becomes a speechmaker deciding at his own discretion the points that he will make.

The danger of this is that speaking from the mind will only reach minds. The preacher whom God uses, however, speaks to the eternal souls of men. Because of this, preparing to preach must start with prayer. In prayer the preacher's spirit is readied at the deepest level. A pastor must pray constantly in the Spirit while reading the Bible and collating the material for a sermon. The Holy Spirit will bring wisdom to the praying pastor's mind and assist him in shaping an inspiring message that will speak to people's hearts.

God's plan for preaching is to speak through "a man sent from God" (John 1:6). It took many years for God to prepare John the Baptist for his unique ministry as Christ's forerunner, and the process worked out in the life of John the Baptist is no different from that of every preacher today. E. M. Bounds said, "It takes twenty years to make a sermon, because it takes twenty years to make the man. The true sermon is a thing of life. The sermon grows because the man grows. The sermon is forceful because the man is forceful. The sermon is holy because the man is holy. The sermon is full of the divine unction because the man is full of the divine unction."[1] Before a man proclaims the message of the Bible to others, he should have prayed over it and then lived with that message himself.

The preacher who is dedicated to prayerfully listening to the Holy Spirit's promptings will be led in the direction that God knows the church needs to go. Over the years I have observed that a particular sermon I had planned months in advance fell on a date when the message was a perfect fit. When that happens, I do not congratulate myself, because I know that only the Holy Spirit could have foreseen the timing.

Prayer enables the preacher to deal with hard issues that require boldness. There must be an element of the prophetic in preaching. In other words, the Word of God must be applied to specific moral issues of the day. The preacher should speak as the oracle of God (see Exodus 4:12; 1 Peter 4:11). Such fearless preaching must be birthed in prayer.

Prayer prepares the preacher's heart to preach. A pastor should never go into the pulpit without having dedicated time alone in prayer. It is wise for a pastor to get alone with God to pray and prepare his heart at least three hours before he preaches.

I have a quiet place for this where I take extended time to meditate and pray. In my preparation prayers I begin with praises to God, and I focus my mind on God's attributes, such as His greatness and His love. I always make sure to confess any sins and to pray that my heart will be right and pure before I preach. Then I move to requests that come to mind about the service or the people who will be leading worship with me. Next I give thanks to God for the miraculous things that He will do in the lives of those who hear His Word preached. Finally, I leave time to be quiet and to listen for the Holy Spirit's promptings. When thoughts come to my mind that are consistent with God's purposes and the Word that I will be preaching, I pray about them and ask God to guide me in how to apply them directly to the service.

An effective preaching pastor must be a praying pastor. Better to preach a simple message carried to people's hearts on the wings of prayer than to preach a complex sermon that falls on deaf ears.

Dedicating the Preacher's Mind Through Practice

An occupational hazard of being a pastor is the mental overload. Every week brings an avalanche of information, follow-up, coordination, planning, counseling, calling, and correspondence. With the blazing speed of today's high-tech communication, I often receive a hundred e-mails every day that require my time. Put all these things together and the pastor's mind can easily become a jumbled mess of conflicting thoughts and pressing obligations.

The Bible cautions us to work on our mental preparation and focus: "Preparing your minds for action, and being sober-minded, set your hope fully on the grace that will be brought to you at the revelation of Jesus Christ" (1 Peter 1:13). "Set your minds on things that are above, not on things that are on earth" (Colossians 3:2). How does a pastor stop the mental overload and focus his mind on things above?

First, the preacher should *prepare his sermons well in advance* of preaching them. Advance preparation allows the mind to marinate on the truths and get comfortable with articulating them. Advance preparation also allows a preacher to mentally work through the hard parts of a sermon until he can communicate them with clarity and confidence.

Second, it helps the preacher to *read through his sermon notes* the night before he preaches. Something good happens when a preacher goes to sleep pondering God's Word. After doing this I have sometimes awakened in the morning with a new insight that connects all the pieces of the sermon in a way that was missing before.

Third, mental preparation means that a preacher should *limit the kinds of activities he does within twenty-four hours of preaching*. He would do well to avoid events and situations that tax the emotions with fear, frustration, anger, or messy relationships. A good rule is to let the mind be still and filled with God before preaching. Psalm 46:10 sets down the simple rule, "Be still, and know that I am God." The preacher with a peaceful, clear, and focused mind will find that his efforts are rewarded.

Dedicating the Preacher's Body Through Personal Care

God cares about the preacher's body, and the preacher should care about it too. One of the blessings of the new birth is that our bodies become the temple of the Holy Spirit (see 1 Corinthians 6:19). Therefore, an effective preacher should pay attention to his body.

A healthy and nourishing diet will balance weight concerns, add strength, and ward off infections and viruses. It is a good idea to avoid overindulging in fatty foods and heavy starches that clog the digestive system. To keep the body healthy, a pastor should eat fruits, vegetables, grains, legumes, and lean meats. The night before he preaches, he should eat well and drink plenty of clean water to cleanse the system. The body is like a living motor that needs clean air, fuel, and water; if we feed it dirty air, dirty food, and dirty water, it will not perform at maximum efficiency.

Preachers who want to maximize their effectiveness must also exercise to stay in shape. Paul wisely says, "Physical training is good, but training for godliness is much better, promising benefits in this life and in the life to come" (1 Timothy 4:8, NLT). Preaching requires a surprising amount of physical and mental energy; it is not uncommon for preachers to feel physically exhausted after preaching. For this reason preachers need to exercise to keep their cardiovascular system at peak performance and to maintain muscle strength. A workout two to three times per week should include brisk walking, running, or jogging to keep the heart and lungs working properly. It helps to add to the weekly routine some isometric exercises or weightlifting to maintain muscle tone.

Taking care of the body provides another important benefit: it helps us live longer and be healthier than we would be otherwise. The average pastor can add years to his life and ministry by consistently eating well and exercising. This is a direct spiritual benefit to taking care of the body.

Think It Over: Dedication of the Preacher for Preaching

1. What part does prayer play in dedicating yourself to God for the task of preaching?
2. How can you do a better job of dedicating your mind so that it is agile and alert when you preach?
3. How can physical fitness enhance your preaching ability?

Interpretation of Scripture for Preaching

The third tool for effective preaching is interpretation of Scripture: "They read from the book, from the Law of God, clearly, and they gave the sense, so that the people understood the reading" (Nehemiah 8:8).

When Ezra read from God's Word to the spiritually starved people of Jerusalem, they listened for hours and then began to weep. The impact of hearing what God had said evoked in them a powerful emotional response because they understood what God meant and how it applied to them. Ezra and the other scribes were not simply reading the Bible; they explained what God's Word meant. This is called interpretation, or the science of hermeneutics.

Biblical hermeneutics is the study of the principles that govern how the text of the Bible should be understood. Hermeneutics is part of a broader field that includes principles of interpretation for all forms of communication, both verbal and nonverbal. I recommend that every preacher utilize eight principles of interpretation.

First, *read and reread the passage*. There is something simple and profound about reading a Bible text over and over. The first reading is like a flyover, the second is like a landing, and the third is like walking through the passage with one's feet on the ground. Many preachers unintentionally fall into errors in doctrine, Bible facts, or the meaning of a text because they don't comprehend what they have read. If a pastor has access to more than one Bible translation, this is a great way to gain a greater grasp and comprehension of a passage.

Second, *identify the type of literature* in the part of Scripture being studied. Bible scholars call this finding the genre of the text. Is the text a narrative story, a prophesy, poetry, history, the gospel, or a letter? The Gospels or Acts constitute a different type of literature than Paul's letters do. The poetry of the Psalms is unique and not like the narratives of the wilderness wanderings in Numbers. A pastoral leader should take care to identify the kind of literature that the Bible writer used to get his message across to the reader.

Third, *understand the context*. Get the big picture or main theme of a text, and then find out how the passage fits together by identifying all its subthemes and ideas. Once a preacher has grasped the immediate context, then he should ask how the text relates to the wider truths of the Bible. This is the most important principle for accurate interpretation. Every Bible truth is like a picture that is understood by the frame that surrounds it. Context takes into consideration the historical, grammatical, social, political, and religious facts that surrounded the time in which the biblical writer was actively writing.

A visual picture of pinpointing context would look like a series of concentric circles, starting with a word in Scripture, then the phrase in which that word is found, then the sentence, the paragraph, the chapter, the book, other books from the same writer, the Old or New Testament, and the entire Bible. Each Bible author follows a logical line of thought in what he writes or tells a story that flows from one scene to the next. When we take a text out of its intended context, we risk misinterpreting it. A preacher should look for clues in the surrounding verses as well. They will help open up the overall meaning of the text. Every clue uncovered is important.

Fourth, *look for the plain and obvious meaning.* The Bible is not full of hidden meanings. The ordinary reading of the text is best. Even though the Bible uses symbolic or figurative language, most of it is clear to the reader. Metaphors, allegories, parables, and prophetic literature can be understood when they are looked at carefully and systematically. It is helpful to know the background of the people, places, or events in order to grasp the plain meaning of a text. These facts can serve as guides to discover the accurate meaning.

Fifth, *discern the writer's intentions for communicating this truth.* Finding the writer's purpose is critical for the expository preacher. A preacher studies the text not primarily to find a sermon in it but to discover the writer's intended message. Uncovering the purpose of the writer ensures that the preacher will understand the text and preach the message that God intends. A cross-reference Bible, concordance, Bible dictionary, or commentary is useful in seeking to understand the author's purpose.

Sixth, *carefully consider the language of the text and how it reveals the text's meaning.* Words carry thoughts, and the words of the text are all we have to help us understand the writer's thoughts. God inspired the Bible down to the smallest details, and that includes the words: "All Scripture is breathed out by God and profitable for teaching, for reproof, for correction, and for training in righteousness" (2 Timothy 3:16). "Truly, I say to you, until heaven and earth pass away, not an iota, not a dot, will pass from the Law until all is accomplished" (Matthew 5:18). The Holy Spirit inspired the Bible authors to use precise words so that we could know the precise messages that God meant to communicate.

The preacher should look closely at the words of a passage, examining each one carefully for the part it plays in the overall message. Many preachers study Greek and Hebrew for this reason. But even if a preacher cannot read the original languages, he can still use lexicons and word-study books to guide him. Though the congregation is probably not interested in the Hebrew and Greek, the preacher's study of words in the original languages will open insights to him that will make the message clearer.

The preacher should look for these key words to unlock the meaning of a text:

- "Therefore"—a summary word or a concluding word at the end of some steps or lines of thought (see Romans 12:1)
- "So that" or "that"—a phrase that unlocks purpose (see John 3:16)
- "In"—reveals close relationship, such as "in Christ" (see 2 Corinthians 5:17)
- "Of" or "from"—denotes origin or source (see 2 Corinthians 5:18)
- "With"—reveals partnership or association (see 1 John 1:3)
- "Through" or "by"—reveals a process or the means by which something is done (see Romans 7:25; 1 Corinthians 15:57)

Along with locating key connecting words that give clues to the meaning of the passage, a preacher can look for the verbs that describe action or a state of being. Here are a few examples:

- "Has"—present possession (see 1 John 5:11–12)
- "Is"—present status (see Philippians 2:5)
- "Will"—future status (see John 3:16, NLT)
- "Had"—past possession (see 1 Peter 2:10)
- "Was"—past status (see Luke 15:32)

Look for conditional phrases that begin with "if" and conclude with a fulfillment, as in 2 Chronicles 7:14 and 1 John 1:9: "*If* my people who are called by my name humble themselves, and pray and seek my face and turn from their wicked ways [four conditions], then I will hear from heaven and will forgive their sin and heal their land [three promises]." Or "*If* we confess our sins [one condition], he is faithful and just to forgive us our sins and to cleanse us from all unrighteousness [two promises]."

Seventh, *identify the main theological themes.* Identifying the theological themes and understanding how they relate to one another in the text is a helpful way to grasp the meaning of the passage. Ask questions like "What does this text teach about the character, the will, or the work of God?" or "To which of the main doctrines does this text speak truth?" (For a list of the main divisions of theology, see appendix 4.)

Eighth and finally, *always take a Christ-centered perspective.* Look at every text to uncover what it reveals about Jesus. Jesus said, "You search the Scriptures because you think that in them you have eternal life; and it is they that bear witness about me" (John 5:39).

What the Bible says about Jesus will always be central to every text. This is why Paul said, "I decided to know nothing among you except Jesus Christ and him crucified" (1 Corinthians 2:2). God has sovereignly chosen to impact both the saved and the unsaved with the person of Christ and His finished work of salvation. Therefore, when the gospel of Jesus is proclaimed, the preacher hits at the heart of what God wants everyone to know.

Think It Over: Interpretation of Scripture for Preaching

1. What did you find most helpful in this section on interpretation? What did you learn about interpreting the passage?
2. Which theological themes do you feel most comfortable preaching on, and which themes need more time in your preaching?

Organization of the Message for Preaching

The fourth tool for scriptural preaching is organization: "If you put these things before the brothers, you will be a good servant of Christ Jesus, being trained in the words of the faith and of the good doctrine that you have followed" (1 Timothy 4:6).

It is up to each pastor whether to use an outline or a manuscript as his preaching notes. The preacher who has the rare ability to memorize his outline will have the greatest amount of freedom. On the subject of sermon notes, there is no rule on whether to use them or not. Many great preachers use an outline or notes or even a full manuscript; others use no notes at all. The decision is up to each preacher.

A sermon should be organized in a particular manner.

First of all, it is important to *keep the main theme in mind while finding the supporting parts*. The first thing a preacher must do to organize the Bible text into a sermon is get the main theme of passage. Finding the main theme is like stepping back to look at the passage as one whole subject from beginning to end. Sometimes it is helpful to ask these questions of the text:

- What major Bible doctrine about God's character, plan, or purposes does this express?
- What part of Christ's life and redemptive work does this emphasize?
- What does this narrative teach about man?

Once the main theme is identified, the next step is to *find the supporting truths*—the individual parts that support the main theme. The smaller parts can be found by asking basic questions like "who, what, when, how, and why. Below are some examples of questions that help lead to the sub-points of the main theme:

- How many truths relate to the main theme?
- Is there a logical order or progression to what God has revealed?
- Does this passage give insight into the reasons that this truth is significant or why it fits into God's plan?
- Who is the main character in the story, and who are the supporting characters?
- What does each character bring to the meaning of the story?
- Has God put a timeframe on when these truths happened in the past or will happen in the future?

After the main theme has been pinpointed and the supporting truths discovered, the preacher should *create an outline with an introduction, main body, and conclusion*. The components of these are detailed step by step below:

Introduction:

- A good introduction should make use of an interesting story, an attention-arresting point, a gripping title, or a humorous illustration to gain the attention of the hearers.
- A well-planned introduction sets the tone for the rest of the message. An introduction should command attention.
- Keep it short. The introduction should only be long enough to capture attention, raise needs, and orient the audience to the subject, idea, or first point. One woman said of the great Welsh preacher John Owen that he was so long spreading the table that she lost her appetite for the meal!
- The introduction should not promise more than it delivers. When the preacher fails to answer the question he has raised or meet the expectation he has aroused, the congregation will feel cheated. Sensational introductions to mediocre sermons resemble broken promises.
- The main theme of the message should be clearly illustrated and stated in the introduction.
- The introduction can hint at the application of the sermon. A good introduction tells the people listening where you want to take them and why it's important that they stay focused as you move into the body of the message.

The body:

- An effective message should have an understandable logical sequence and progression. The sermon should be easy to follow and remember.
- Unless a sermon is memorable, it is of limited value. Most people want to remember what the preacher says; therefore it is the preacher's responsibility to assist them.
- Effective sermons maintain a sense of tension. They do not give away everything at the beginning. Good sermons build and lead the hearers in a progressively unfolding plot.

- Transitional ideas are critical, because they connect the various points of the sermon. Good transitions enable the message to flow and not seem disconnected or disorganized.
- The body of the sermon should be filled with sub-points that illustrate, develop, or explain the main theme.
- Good sermons do not overburden listeners with too many sub-points.
- Each of the sub-points should be titled to give them clarity. The use of alliteration or associated titles will help organize the message and give it clarity.
- Stories or illustrations from the listeners' general knowledge can lead them from the known to the unknown or from the natural to the spiritual. The preacher should give specific attention to illustrating the points that he is making. Clear illustrations make it easier for the congregation to understand and remember the message as a whole.
- Each point should be a statement, not a question. The points of the sermon outline should answer questions, not raise them. However, questions may be used in the delivery of the sermon as transitions to introduce new points.
- Whenever possible, a preacher should lead the audience in the self-discovery of truth by implying a point rather than stating it directly. When a preacher says something directly, it is simply not as potent as when he allows people to discover it for themselves.

Conclusion:

- Every sermon needs a conclusion.
- Just as an airplane pilot needs special planning and concentration to land his craft at a pre-designated point, so the skillful preacher should never be in doubt about where or how his sermon will land.
- Some outstanding preachers treat this part of the message so seriously that they prepare it first. The conclusion should produce a feeling of finality and allow the minister to call for a verdict from

the people. Either directly or indirectly, the conclusion of the message should answer the questions raised in the message and make the people face another question: "What am I going to do about this?" "Am I willing for God to work this into my life?" etc.

- The conclusion should make a smooth progression to an altar call or decision time that will enable the sermon to be acted upon.

Think It Over: Organization of the Message for Preaching

1. What method do you use to prepare your notes and organize your thoughts for your sermons?
2. Which part of organizing a message is most challenging for you: choosing a main theme, finding supporting truths, or creating an outline with an introduction, body, and conclusion? How can you improve in this area?

Proclamation for Powerful Preaching

The fifth step to powerful and effective preaching is proclamation: "Preach the word; be ready in season and out of season; reprove, rebuke, and exhort, with complete patience and teaching" (2 Timothy 4:2).

Adequate personal preparation and dedication, sound interpretation, and great organization are like the launching pad for a missile—they prepare the sermon for liftoff! But once these steps have been taken, the preacher must turn his attention to actually proclaiming the message that God has given him.

How can a preacher give a great delivery? There is no simple answer to that question, but several factors will help take a great sermon from words on a page or thoughts in a pastor's memory to a powerful life-changing message through which God touches someone with eternal truth.

Use Body Language

Communication studies show that 93 percent of what we convey is unspoken. This dominant nonverbal part of any communication includes both body language and tone of voice. The preacher should take care to develop skills that improve his tone and body language.

During a message's introduction an audience gains impressions of a speaker that often determine whether or not they will accept what he says. If he appears nervous, hostile, or unprepared, they are inclined to reject him. If he seems alert, friendly, and interesting, the listeners decide that he is an able person with a positive attitude toward himself and his listeners. Some preachers mistakenly think that shouting and screaming will improve people's ability to comprehend the message. However, continuous shouting shuts down good communication and eventually makes people tune out. Sometimes the best way to emphasize a point is to lower the voice to a whisper.

Both excessive pacing like a wildcat or standing still like a statue hinder good communication. Natural hand gestures as well as body movements that fit the moment make the proclamation interesting and help maintain the attention of the listeners.

Never Be Dull

When preachers are dull, it says that they did not care enough about their hearers to get the fire and truth from God and package it attractively. Charles Spurgeon, called the "prince of preachers," said this: "Jesus' preaching was attractive. He was too earnest to be dull and too humane to be incomprehensible." Every preacher must develop a vivid style of speaking that will enable a congregation to "experience" the message.

Communication that taps a listener's experience appeals to both mind and feelings. Vividness develops when we let nouns and verbs carry our meaning. When used effectively, strong nouns and verbs will heighten people's level of interest. A "tall man" should become "a giant of a man" or "tall as a basketball player." Instead of saying "he said," use more vivid language like "he roared" or "he thundered." Don't say "he walked," but use more vivid language like "he paced" or "he strolled."

Good sermons use active verbs to make sentences come alive. Passive verbs suck the life out of speech. Verbs, like nouns, wake up the imagination when they are precise. He "went" gets him there, but not as clearly as "crawled," "stumbled," "shuffled," "lurched." She "shouts," "shrieks," "rants," or "whispers" engages the listener with far greater interest than "said" does.

Make the Message Clear

If the message is garbled, the response will be weak or even negative: "If the bugle gives an indistinct sound, who will get ready for battle?" (1 Corinthians 14:8). History records that Napoleon, the great French military general, had three commands for his messengers: "Be clear! Be clear! Be clear!"

The story is told of President Calvin Coolidge returning home from a church service one Sunday and being asked by his wife what the minister had talked about. Coolidge replied, "Sin." When his wife pressed him as to what the preacher had said about sin, Coolidge responded with a note of humor, "I think he was against it." It goes without saying that this is not the kind of response a pastor wants from his hearers. A pastor must present truth clearly so that his congregation will know with certainty the message God is bringing through him.

Develop Storytelling Skills

Learn to tell stories effectively and to paint pictures with words and tone of voice. Package the message in illustrated form.

The prophet Nathan used a story to break through to King David about his hidden sin with Bathsheba (see 2 Samuel 12:1–13). Telling stories within a sermon describes the individuals and events from the biblical accounts. Every passage has its people—sometimes they are laughing, cursing, praying; other times they are hiding in the text, and we must look for them. In every text, though, there is always somebody writing and somebody reading. Pull aside a doctrine, and we find personalities. For example, grace does not exist in cold storage in heaven. There is someone giving grace and someone else receiving it.

The Holy Spirit knew the value of narration, because He filled the Scriptures with stories. Jesus too demonstrated the impact of storytelling in the parables He told.

Narration helps supply background in a sermon by filling in the history, setting, or personalities involved in a text.

Use Illustrations and Humor

Examples or illustrations are like windows that let the light of God's truth into a message. It is a mistake to use only abstract, theoretical, or technical information. Illustrative stories aid memory, stir emotion, create need, hold attention, and establish rapport between the speaker and the hearer.

Good pulpit communication moves back and forth from the abstract to the concrete. Each time the preacher states a broad general truth, the mind of the hearer asks, *For instance?* That's when the preacher needs some example or incident that illustrates the point. Draw illustrations from life, from books, from history, from science, from current events, and from biblical examples.

The best humor comes from real-life situations. A pastor should avoid silly, suggestive, and negative humor. Put-down humor is not appropriate. On the other hand, it is perfectly fine for a pastor to make himself the point of the humor. This helps get the preacher off a pedestal and be seen as anyone else in the audience.

Know the Audience

Learn to be successful in knowing the audience by observing and listening to people. The preacher should find out all he can about his audience's needs, aspirations, and desires. Profiling an audience will enable a preacher to connect with people at their level.

Use Steady Pacing

People speak at a pace of 120–180 words a minute, but most individuals think at least five times faster than that. This is why the attention of listeners tends to wander. The preacher must adjust the delivery and style of his message to the level of his congregation. Speaking too fast will frustrate listeners, and speaking too slowly will put them to sleep. A pastor must learn to change the pace, tone, and volume of his message to keep everyone alert and focused.

Develop Eye Contact

Eyes communicate. The pastor's eyes hold an audience's attention, and the congregation's eyes supply feedback to the pastor. Some people actually choose to sit in the front rows because they want to see the emotion in the preacher's eyes. When a pastor looks directly at his hearers, he picks up clues from their eyes that tell him whether they understand what he is saying, whether they are interested in the message, and whether they are enjoying the sermon enough to continue listening.

Audiences feel that preachers who look them in the eye want to talk with them personally. Therefore, pastors who gaze over people's heads, stare down at notes, look out windows, or worse, shut their eyes while they speak, are at a crippling disadvantage. Almost without exception, a congregation will not listen attentively to a speaker who does not look at them while he talks. Audiences mistrust a speaker who avoids eye contact, and as a result, they undervalue what he says.

An important communication principle helps the pastor here: the preacher addresses a congregation as a group, but he talks to them as individuals. When a pastor stands to speak, he should pause to establish personal contact with his hearers. He should move his eyes over the congregation and let them rest for an instant on several different people. Throughout the sermon he should continue his eye contact. He can plan to talk with one listener at a time for a second or two, looking that person in the eye, then turn to someone else. It is a good idea to choose listeners in every section of the auditorium and to keep eye contact with each one long enough so that they know that the pastor has singled them out and is speaking to them. If the congregation is very large, a preacher can select a small group in one area and look at them for a moment or two, then shift to another group, and continue to do that throughout the sermon.

Stay in the Moment

The preacher can lose his focus even while he is preaching. It is a strange thing about the human brain, but sometimes we attempt to double-task and lose our focus. This can become a spiritual battle that reveals itself in distractions that draw the preacher's attention away from the message: a crying baby, a sudden noise, or a nagging fly buzzing around can redirect a pastor's thinking and dilute his concentration. Sometimes it is a physical problem that arises while preaching, like an upset stomach, a leg cramp, or a dry mouth.

These annoyances can draw the preacher's thoughts and attention away from his message. When this happens, passion and focus can be lost, and the sermon loses its potential impact. A preacher is like an athlete who must discipline his mind not to wander. Staying in the moment is an important discipline for the effective preacher.

To some extent the preacher is part of the message. Therefore, he can enable clear communication by avoiding some distracting flaws:

- *Attitude*—never be careless or flippant with God's Word. People will see it and question your heart!
- *Dress*—develop the habit of dressing in a neat and inspiring way. Allowing for differences in style and taste, three traits are common: having hair neat, the body clean, and clothes that fit the cultural style.
- *Mannerisms*—avoid all offensive mannerisms that will take the hearers' attention away from the message. Stuffing hands in the pockets, stroking the hair or face, playing with a ring, fussing with a necktie, and shuffling the feet are annoying distractions. A preacher can overcome distracting habits by inviting feedback from his congregation and trusted church leaders and by listening to audio recordings or watching video recordings of his own preaching.
- *Poor grammar and use of language*—since the message is couched in words, the diligent preacher will do all in his power to use them correctly. People tend to subconsciously correct the preacher's bad grammar, pronunciation, and emphasis. When the audience is correcting the bad grammar of the preacher, they are losing their concentration on the message. Poor grammar and faulty pronunciation unnerve a listener and raise doubts about the preacher's competence.
- *Length of the sermon*—the mind cannot assimilate more than the seat can endure! Stop speaking before people get disinterested or distracted. Fredrick Temple, archbishop of Canterbury in the late nineteenth century, was a humane, liberal, and sensible man. It is said that he once remarked, "In making a sermon, think up a good beginning, then think up a good ending, then bring these two as close together as you can." An appropriate prayer could be, "Lord, fill my mouth with worthwhile stuff, and nudge me when I've said enough."

Think It Over: Proclamation for Powerful Preaching

1. What did you learn about proclamation that will help you preach better in the future?
2. How would you rate your storytelling skill? How can you improve that skill?
3. How would you rate your use of body language, gestures, eye contact, pace, and vocal tone?
4. What mannerisms do you have that may distract from the message?
5. What is your plan to get some feedback on how your preaching is being received? Ask a trusted friend? Record yourself?

Application of the Preaching

The sixth tool for effective preaching is leading people to an application of the message: "Be doers of the word, and not hearers only, deceiving yourselves" (James 1:22).

One of the best pieces of advice that I can give to a preacher is to preach for a verdict. It is not enough for people to get more information about God; they need to be moved to act on what they have heard. This is often effected by an altar call, or an invitation.

Billy Graham candidly stated, "At the invitation there is a great spiritual conflict. This is the part of the evangelistic service that wears me out physically and psychologically and spiritually more than any other. I sense that Satan is battling for the souls of men."[2] At the point of the altar call, the spiritual conflict of the universe between good and evil, between the forces of darkness and the God of light, arrives. At that moment unsaved people's eyes can be opened so that they can "turn from darkness to light and from the power of Satan to God, that they may receive forgiveness of sins" (Acts 26:18), and Christians can be convicted to reject the old self and embrace again the new self, "created after the likeness of God in true righteousness and holiness" (Ephesians 4:24).

On Sunday, October 8, 1871, before the great Chicago fire broke out that evening, D. L. Moody preached in Farwell Hall on the text "What Will You Do with Jesus Who Is Called the Christ?" He then urged his audience to consider his message that week and to think about choosing Christ when they returned the following Sunday. That night the place where Moody had preached burned to the ground and so did his home and most of Chicago. Many people lost their lives in the fire and never returned to church. Later Moody said that telling people to come back in a week to make a decision for Christ was the worst mistake he ever made. He determined from that experience to always make the message of salvation plain and then lovingly encourage spiritual decisions at that moment.

It is uncertain how the term "altar call" originated, but the practice of calling for a decision to be made as a result of the preaching is valid. A moment of decision happened on the Day of Pentecost when the Holy Spirit came and Peter rose up and declared the gospel in power. When Peter finished preaching, he called the people to make a decision: "Repent and be baptized every one of you in the name of Jesus Christ for the forgiveness of your sins, and you will receive the gift of the Holy Spirit. For the promise is for you and for your children and for all who are far off, everyone whom the Lord our God calls to himself" (Acts 2:38–39).

In fact, the Bible is filled with examples of invitations being made for hearers to respond to the Lord. Moses confronted the people of Israel with their idolatry and pressed them for a verdict: "Who is on the Lord's side? Come to me" (Exodus 32:26). Joshua, at the end of his life fearing that Israel would backslide, told the people, "Choose this day whom you will serve, whether the gods your fathers served in the region beyond the River, or the gods of the Amorites in whose land you dwell. But as for me and my house, we will serve the Lord" (Joshua 24:15). When the people responded, Joshua recorded their decision in the book of the law of God and erected a stone "decision card" as a witness to their response (see Joshua 24:26–27). The Lord Jesus set the same example, preaching, "The time is fulfilled, and the kingdom of God is at hand; repent and believe in the gospel" (Mark 1:15). To Peter and Andrew, He called, "Follow me, and I will make you become fishers of men" (Mark 1:17). Jesus often said, "Repent," "Believe," "Come," "Choose." Merely preaching facts that do not call for or compel a decision is like fishing with the finest bait and tackle and then failing to land the fish.

Staggering though it may seem, God is calling people through the preacher today. "We are ambassadors for Christ, God making his appeal through us. We implore you on behalf of Christ, be reconciled to God" (2 Corinthians 5:20). In light of this, to what kind of spiritual decisions are preachers to call people? The pastor's responsibility is twofold. First, he is to *call the lost to Christ*: "Do the work of an evangelist, fulfill your ministry" (2 Timothy 4:5).

Regardless of whether the preacher considers himself to be an evangelist, all preachers must call sinners to Christ. Overwhelming evidence shows that more people come to Christ and stand firm in their faith through the regular ministry of the local church than through evangelistic crusades. The pastor will need to break through the barrier of feeling incapable and believe God for souls in his ministry, being bold to overcome his natural reticence. He must pray and believe for this to occur whenever he preaches. He should not give up for lack of results initially. Biblical preachers call for decisions.

Below are ten guidelines in conducting an appeal for salvation decisions:

- *Plan for it.* The preacher should spend a considerable time in preparation and prayer for the altar call. This is almost as important as the message. The preacher who waits on God in prayer and makes plans for an altar call will discover that the altar call will fall into place, and he will not hastily discard it at the end of the service when he is under emotional stress or feeling drained.
- *Be sensitive.* Sense the mood of the meeting and the leading of the Holy Spirit. Learn to be "in the moment" and to know the nudging of the Holy Spirit. At times the appeal can even precede the preaching. Not every sermon lends itself to a call to the unsaved. Be led by the Spirit.
- *Be flexible.* Avoid being predictable. Invite people to identify their decisions in a variety of ways such as raising their hand, standing to their feet, walking forward, or audibly repeating a prayer.
- *Be specific.* Spell out clearly what you are appealing for, and make it absolutely plain what you want the respondents to do. You may call for different needs in succession. Some messages directed at Christians are meant to call them to serve, repent of certain sins, or dedicate themselves to a particular plan of action. Be clear as to what you are asking of the listeners.

- *Establish contact.* Do not let people slip away without having made a personal contact with you or a trained counselor. It is essential that the unsaved make a specific profession of faith (see Romans 10:9) and that Christians make a specific dedication (see Romans 12:1–2).
- *Pray with and for people.* Lead unsaved respondents in a specific prayer renouncing their sins, asking for forgiveness, and inviting Jesus to be their Savior and Lord. Always include a faith element by having them verbally declare that Jesus is now their Lord and Savior (see Romans 10:9–10). Praying with and for Christians will seal their decision too. No one who responds to the altar call should go away without prayer.
- *Have trained counselors.* The counselors should be ready to meet those who respond to the invitation. Respondents should be counseled in a place that is free from distraction. Counselors should be familiar with the follow-up procedures of the local church.
- *Use music and singers during the appeal.* Music is a God-given facility for conveying the touch of the Spirit to the human heart. In 1 Chronicles 25:1, 2 Chronicles 20:22, and 2 Kings 3:15, we find that praise to God is conducive to encouraging a spiritual response in the hearers.
- *Be loving.* Never be offensive or manipulative. Do not expose or embarrass people. Be considerate and courteous. Put yourself in their place.
- *Don't be in a hurry, but don't drag it out.* Long appeals will weary the people and turn them off rather than draw them in. Have faith that the Holy Spirit is doing His convicting work in the congregation, and if there is no response in a reasonable time, don't feel uncomfortable about dismissing the congregation. On the other hand, respect the work of the Holy Spirit and be patient while He is working.

Whenever he preaches, the pastor should expect the convicting power of the Holy Spirit to be present to produce real repentance. Only the Holy Spirit can convict a lost soul of his sin and lead him to repentance. Jesus said, "No one can come to me unless the Father who sent me draws him" (John 6:44). Repentance is a gift given through God's sovereign grace to sinful people by the Holy Spirit (see Acts 11:18; 16:14). Spirit-anointed preaching is a method used by God to strike conviction into the hearts of sinners and professed Christians alike.

The second responsibility of a pastor in calling for decisions is to *call believers to commitment*: "I appeal to you therefore, brothers, by the mercies of God, to present your bodies as a living sacrifice, holy and acceptable to God, which is your spiritual worship" (Romans 12:1). During a time of great spiritual need, fifteenth-century preacher Savonarola, under the anointing of the Spirit, fearlessly raising his voice in condemnation of sin in pleasure-mad Florence, Italy. The church had become so corrupt that Savonarola stood alone in his preaching. As large crowds came to hear him, at Savonarola's invitation, tears ran freely, and people beat their breasts and cried to God for mercy.

Similarly, during the Great Awakening in America, Jonathan Edwards preached his famous sermon "Sinners in the Hands of an Angry God." Historians reported that people actually grasped hold of pillars and pews because they felt that they were sliding into the pit of hell! Evangelist John Wesley was denied the use of the church in which his father had pastored for forty years, so he stood on his father's tombstone outside the church and preached the gospel. Conviction became so intense that at times his voice was drowned out by the cries of the penitents and the sound of weeping. Consider George Whitfield preaching to ten thousand coal miners in England. As the Word of God penetrated their hearts, streams of tears washed their soot-covered cheeks.

Finally, after the preacher has done everything he knows to do, he must leave the rest to God. Not everyone will be saved, and not every Christian will obey the call to complete surrender to Christ. Ultimately, people's salvation is not up to the preacher; it is up to the Lord. Jesus said to His Father, "I glorified you on earth, having accomplished the work that you gave me to do" (John 17:4). Jesus did not heal all the sick, feed all the poor, or raise all the dead. He did what God had ordained for Him to do. The preacher is called to do what God has ordained—nothing more, nothing less, nothing else.

Think It Over: Application of the Preaching

1. What can you do to make the altar call more effective and organized?
2. Who in your congregation can you train as counselors to minister to those who respond to your altar call?

Preservation of the Preaching

The seventh and final tool for powerful biblical preaching is preservation: "The one who looks into the perfect law, the law of liberty, and perseveres, being no hearer who forgets but a doer who acts, he will be blessed in his doing" (James 1:25).

People need to remember the Word of God in order to live it out. Preachers today have some great advantages over preachers in previous times, since in our day sermons can live on to bless and challenge many people over and over. For starters, preachers can print their messages in pamphlets and books for distribution or publishing. Today's self-publishing is very different than in the world before computers and print-on-demand options. Posting a printed sermon online requires only a few computer clicks.

Some large churches have access to recording devices that can capture sermons in audio. Once the sermon is recorded, it can be recorded on a CD, made into a Podcast, or even aired on radio. With reproduction costs going down, sermon CDs can be offered at very reasonable costs.

People also have ways to capture sermons in video. In times past it was financially impossible for a preacher to distribute his sermons in video, but today a preacher can post his sermon on web-based platforms like YouTube, Facebook, or Livestream. The opportunities for sermons to have increased impact worldwide are abundant.

Think It Over: Preservation of the Preaching

1. What plans do you have to preserve the sermons you give so that they can be read, heard, or seen again?
2. Who are some people who could benefit directly from having your sermons in written, audio, or visual form?

CONCLUSION:
The Pastoral Leader and Preaching

A strong pulpit ministry generates a strong church, even if everything else is lacking. God's sovereign plan is to use preaching to reach the world for Christ. God's plan is to use men as preachers. "How are they to preach unless they are sent? As it is written, 'How beautiful are the feet of those who preach the good news!'" (Romans 10:15). What an amazing God!

7

The Pastoral Leader and the Great Commission

Objective: *To define the gospel as well as the motives, means, message, messengers, and map for accomplishing the Great Commission.*

If the Bible was summarized, its most basic message would be the amazing history of God's gracious plan to reconcile humanity (His lost and sinful creation who were made in His image) to Himself through faith in Jesus Christ (God's only Son who was miraculously born of a virgin, died on the cross for all sin, and rose from the dead to prove His power over sin, death, and condemnation). A summary of the gospel would also include God's gracious offer of new life and eternal salvation that is free and meant for all nations (see Mark 16:15; Ephesians 2:8–9).

When the apostle Paul reduced the gospel to its most basic parts, he put it this way: "I delivered to you as of first importance what I also received: that Christ died for our sins in accordance with the Scriptures, that he was buried, that he was raised on the third day in accordance with the Scriptures" (1 Corinthians 15:3–4). Paul tied the gospel to the fulfillment of God's promises to send the Messiah—the Savior predicted by the Jewish prophets in the Scriptures.

Christ's death, burial, and resurrection constitute the most basic message of good news to the world. Why? Because the universal consequence of sin for mankind is death and separation from God forever (see Romans 6:23). The gospel is good news because it is the fulfillment of God's loving intent to rescue eternally lost and dying humanity.

God has progressively revealed His plan to save lost humanity, but every stage in His revelation points to the ultimate fulfillment of our salvation in Jesus Christ. God first revealed His plan to send a Savior in the Old Testament, in Genesis 3. In the garden of Eden, immediately after Adam and Eve's fall into sin (see Genesis 3:1–7), God made a stunning promise: He would one day send a Savior. As Adam and Eve listened, covered with shame, God declared His redemptive plan to save humanity in His words of condemnation to Satan: "I will put enmity between you and the woman, and between your offspring and her offspring; he shall bruise your head, and you shall bruise his heel" (Genesis 3:15).

From this prophetic promise we learn three astounding truths:

- God's plan of redemption for mankind included the destruction of Satan and the complete conquest of evil: "He [Christ, the offspring of the woman] shall *bruise your head* [a death blow]."
- God promised to use the offspring of the woman in order to fulfill His plan to put an end to evil and rescue sinners: "I will put enmity between you and the woman, and between your offspring and *her offspring*."
- The offspring of the woman would crush Satan's head with a deathblow but in doing so would suffer a painful wound: "You [Satan] shall *bruise his heel* [Christ's painful death on the cross]."

This first promise of salvation in Genesis 3:15 looked forward to Christ, who was born of the virgin Mary—the miraculous offspring of the woman. Christ's bruising death on the cross delivered a crushing blow to Satan and to sin. It rendered judgment on Satan and offered eternal salvation to fallen mankind. The hope of the gospel is contained in this first promise of the Messiah. God's plan of salvation predated the creation of the world (see Ephesians 1:4), and He revealed it to man after man's fall into sin. It has always been God's loving plan to save lost people.

Throughout the Old Testament God continued to reveal more details of His plan of salvation. Noah preached repentance for 120 years, warning humanity of God's coming judgment for sin. In the end only Noah and his family were saved through the ark that God had designed and Noah had built (see Genesis 6–8). Noah's salvation from God's judgment through an ark of safety is clearly a picture of Christ, who is our ark of salvation.

Next God spoke to Abraham and made three specific promises to him: God promised Abraham a land; He told him that he would father a nation through a son to be born; and He declared that Abraham would be a blessing through his offspring to all the nations of the world (see Genesis 12:1–3). God focused the lens of His plan on a place (Canaan), a family (the Jews), and a coming descendant of Abraham (Jesus Christ) to bless all people.

Later, under the Mosaic law, God pictured His plan of salvation through types seen in the priesthood and in the tabernacle. But the most dramatic image God gave was that seen in the Passover (see Exodus 12:1–51). Through God's miraculous deliverance of Israel from slavery in Egypt, striking new details were added to the portrait of God's plan of salvation. God's plan required that a young male lamb without blemish be slain at twilight (see Exodus 12:2–6). The blood of that lamb was to be applied to the doorposts of the household, and the people inside were commanded to eat the roasted flesh of the lamb with unleavened bread and bitter herbs (see Exodus 12:7–10). All the lamb was to be eaten, and the lamb's bones were not to be broken (see Exodus 12:46). God promised life only to those who believed and obeyed His plan of deliverance (see Exodus 12:12–13). The Passover feast stands forever as a remembrance of God's rescue from death and slavery (see Exodus 12:14), but it also looks forward as a portrait of Christ's redemptive death. In the Passover God's plan of salvation was revealed with remarkable details that find exclusive fulfillment in Jesus Christ.

The progressive revelation of God's plan of salvation continued during the period of conquest under Joshua (see Joshua 4:19–24), in God's promise of an heir and an eternal throne to King David (see 2 Samuel 7), and in the detailed predictions of the prophets (see Isaiah 7:14; 9:6–7; 53:1–6; Micah 5:2). The sweep of the entire Old Testament looks forward to the coming of Jesus, the Messiah.

Jesus Himself declared that He was the central theme of the Old Testament: "Beginning with Moses and all the Prophets, he interpreted to them in all the Scriptures the things concerning himself" (Luke 24:27). Therefore the gospel centers on Jesus Christ—His person, His redemptive work, and His offer to us of eternal life through our faith in Him.

After Jesus rose from the dead, He spoke the Great Commission to His disciples on five different occasions. In each instance He gave different aspects as to what the Great Commission includes.

In Matthew 28:18–20 Jesus told His followers to "make disciples of all nations" by baptizing them and teaching them to obey the gospel. Mark 16:15 and 19–22 states that they were to "proclaim the gospel to the whole creation," making clear that the message is for all people. Luke 24:46–49 makes it clear that the Great Commission was to be undertaken specifically by those who had walked with Jesus through His sufferings—those who were "witnesses of these things." In John 17:18 and 20:21–23 Jesus said, "As the Father has sent me, so I am sending you"—in other words, into a world that hates light and loves darkness. And in Acts 1:8 Jesus made it clear that the Great Commission is to be done in His power, not man's: "You will receive power when the Holy Spirit has come upon you."

From these five statements in Scripture we can work out a definition of the Great Commission: the Great Commission is God's global purpose to use God's people to proclaim God's salvation in God's power to lost people whom God loves.

It has been over two thousand years since our gloriously resurrected Savior claimed all authority in heaven and Earth. Based on that authority, Jesus gave His disciples their marching orders to make disciples of all nations. Since that time the advance of the gospel has experienced great movements as well as at times paralysis through neglect, distraction, or outright disobedience by the church. In the twenty-first century, the church faces a new challenge to get the gospel out to the world. The need has never been greater. Consider these statistics:

- Less than half of the world's population has been evangelized.
- Less than one-third of the world's population is even nominally Christian.
- Thousands of hidden people groups have never heard the gospel.
- There are over one billion Muslims in the world.

With so many people to be reached, the current challenge seems overwhelming. We know, however, that God loves the world and is "not wishing that any should perish" (2 Peter 3:9). The facts indicate that at the beginning of the twenty-first century, God is orchestrating a huge spiritual harvest. More people are coming to faith in Jesus Christ today than at any other time in history. Statistically speaking, if every Christian on Earth today evangelized one person per year, the Great Commission would be accomplished in about three years! This is why it is crucial that the twenty-first-century church needs to reemphasize the Great Commission.

The Motives for Obeying the Great Commission

The Great Commission finds its source in the heart of God. God was so full of love for lost humanity that it motivated Him to send His Son to redeem mankind and offer sinners new life. His love for the lost should likewise motivate us to share the gospel with those around us who do not know Christ.

The Love of God

Everything about the Great Commission has to do with love. God's love is where the plan of salvation started (see John 3:16; 1 John 4:9-11), God's love is what motivated Jesus to die for man's sins (see Galatians 2:20), God's love moved Him to offer salvation as a free gift (see Romans 5:8; Ephesians 2:4-5), and God's love should motivate us when we communicate the gospel to others (see 2 Corinthians 5:14; 1 Thessalonians 2:8).

The love of God is the greatest thing in the universe. It far exceeds any measurement that anyone could use. Before the Great Commission can be adequately understood, it needs to be seen in the light of the infinite love of God. This is why Paul prayed that the believers in Ephesus would "have strength to comprehend with all the saints what is the breadth and length and height and depth, and to know the love of Christ that surpasses knowledge" (Ephesians 3:18-19). Any motivation less than love is inadequate when sharing the good news of Jesus Christ. Love is what should motivate the Christian to obey the Great Commission, "for the love of Christ controls us" (2 Corinthians 5:14).

The Lost Condition of Man

The lost condition of man prompted Jesus to leave the glories of heaven, and it should cause us to leave our comfort zones as well.

The incarnation of Christ shows us how far Jesus was ready to go to identify Himself with lost humanity. Jesus intentionally experienced all the struggles and temptations that we do. He identified with us so that He could be a sympathetic mediator between us and the Father: "We do not have a high priest who is unable to sympathize with our weaknesses, but one who in every respect has been tempted as we are, yet without sin" (Hebrews 4:15).

It is not enough for pastors to feel sorry for the hopeless plight of the lost, the least, and the last. Christians' pity for the lost will not save them. But God *will* use His servants' obedient action to reach the world. How many missions have been started by Christians who were willing to identify themselves with the broken condition of those around them? As these believers stepped out in obedience, God used their mission to reach the lost with the gospel. Man's lost condition and human struggles are a motive for us to boldly step out to fulfill the Great Commission.

The New Life Offered by Jesus Christ

If you had a cure for cancer and kept it to yourself, how might people dying of cancer think of you? They certainly would not applaud your silence or your selfish failure to act. What believers are commanded to share is far greater than a cure for cancer. Eternal life through Jesus Christ is much more than a temporary fix for an earthly disease. Jesus promised those who believe in Him a new life that is abundant and lasts forever (see John 6:40; 10:10). God's gracious gift of salvation exceeds and outlasts anything that this world has to offer, and God has given us the privilege and duty to be His ambassadors to share this new life with those who are dying eternally without Christ (see 2 Corinthians 5:17–21).

When the Bible translators finally delivered a copy of the Bible in the language of the Kabyle people of northern Algeria, they asked, "What took you so long? We have been having dreams and visions about Jesus for a long time." The reality of new life in Christ offered freely to lost people is a powerful motivation for us to fulfill the Great Commission.

Think It Over: The Motives for Obeying the Great Commission

1. How will the unsaved people around you know that God loves them?
2. What should be your approach with unbelievers, since you know that God loves them?

3. How does the lost condition of sinners impact you most often? Discuss.
   a. Lost people annoy me.
   b. I pity lost people.
   c. I try to avoid lost people.
   d. Lost people motivate me to share my faith.
   e. Other ________________
4. What is the best thing about your new life in Christ that makes you want to share it with others?

The Means of Fulfilling the Great Commission

While pastoral leaders are called to share the gospel, God has given certain means by which the job is to be done. The work done in man's strength will not succeed; it must be done with God's help through prayer, the empowering of the Holy Spirit, and anointed preaching and witnessing.

Prayer

Prayer lays the foundation of any great work that God decides to do. On the Day of Pentecost, the 120 disciples gathered in the upper room were praying when the Holy Spirit filled them. The evidence of the Holy Spirit's filling was power for witnessing (see Acts 1:8).

The role of prayer is central in breaking down the barriers of ignorance and unbelief. Spiritually blind people need the miracle of the Spirit's illuminating work in order to see and believe (see 1 Corinthians 2:14). This is why Paul urged the Colossian believers to pray for an open door for the gospel among the prisoners where he was being held. Prayer opens the door to lost people.

Prayer also prepares the messenger to take the message to the lost. Paul asked the Colossians to pray for him to make the message clear and to speak as he ought to (see Colossians 4:3–4). Prayer has the power to shape the words of God's messenger so that lost people can hear and understand them. Jesus taught His disciples the importance of prayer in fulfilling the Great Commission in Matthew 9:37–38 when He said to them, "The harvest is plentiful, but the laborers are few; therefore pray earnestly to the Lord of the harvest to send out laborers into his harvest." God ordained prayer as one of the means to carry out His work in reaching the lost with the good news of salvation in Jesus Christ.

Power of the Holy Spirit

The Lord Jesus asked the disciples to wait in Jerusalem until they were filled with the Holy Spirit before taking the gospel to the world. He knew that without the power of the Holy Spirit, they would not be effective witnesses for Him. They needed the Holy Spirit for strength and boldness to face opposition.

Before the Holy Spirit came at Pentecost, the disciples had fled in fear and denied Jesus during His trial. Their behavior is shocking, since these same disciples had listened to all Jesus' teachings and seen His miracles. Later they also witnessed His resurrection, but without the Holy Spirit, they did not have the power to witness. Jesus told them that they needed to wait until the Holy Spirit came and anointed them with power before they could witness for Him (see Acts 1:8). After the disciples received the Holy Spirit, however, they boldly declared the good news about Jesus (see Acts 2:5–12), they were willing to suffer for Christ (see Acts 5:40–41), and they were willing to joyfully die as martyrs for Jesus (see Acts 7).

The only way that the Great Commission can be fulfilled in our time is for believers to be filled with the Holy Spirit and power. Only then will today's disciples be bold witnesses for Jesus (see 2 Timothy 1:7). The absence of boldness to witness in many Christians today is directly related to the lack of filling with the Holy Spirit. Paul credited his successful ministry among the Gentiles to the powerful working of God (see Ephesians 3:7). Success in fulfilling the Great Commission today will be directly connected to the powerful working of the Holy Spirit.

The Holy Spirit not only empowers the messenger to bear fruit (see Acts 1:8), but He also brings the conviction of sin, righteousness, and coming judgment to the unbeliever (see John 16:8–11). Jesus said that no one can come to salvation in Him unless the Father draws him (see John 6:44). Christians must learn not to rely on their persuasive skills but on the Holy Spirit to convict the hearts of sinners. Unbelievers cannot comprehend spiritual truth without the help of the Holy Spirit (see

1 Corinthians 2:14). Christians must never attempt to usurp the work of the Holy Spirit by accusing and condemning sinners in hopes of producing conviction of sin.

The first thing unbelievers need to hear is the message of God's love and compassion, because "God's kindness is meant to lead [people] to repentance" (Romans 2:4). Jesus always spoke to sinners with disarming kindness. He was called the friend of sinners (see Matthew 11:19). Sinners were drawn to Jesus by the Holy Spirit's work, and many repented of their sins and became His most devoted followers.

Preaching the Gospel and Bearing Witness to It

God ordained that preaching and bearing witness should be the means of spreading the gospel. Preaching is described in 1 Corinthians 1:21: "Since, in the wisdom of God, the world did not know God through wisdom, it pleased God through the folly of what we preach to save those who believe," and in Acts 1:8 Jesus also said that His disciples would be His witnesses to the entire world.

After Pentecost the early Christians followed Christ's example of preaching and His command to be His witnesses as their pattern of spreading the gospel: "Every day, in the temple and from house to house, they did not cease teaching and preaching that the Christ is Jesus" (Acts 5:42).

Think It Over: The Means of Fulfilling the Great Commission

1. What part does prayer play in fulfilling the Great Commission?
2. For whose salvation are you praying right now? For what community? Region? Nation?
3. What will you do to raise awareness for the need of prayer in your church?
4. Why shouldn't you try to witness without the Holy Spirit?
5. What does the Holy Spirit do that only He can do in the sharing of the gospel?
6. What role does preaching have in advancing the gospel?
7. Why did God choose preaching as the means of taking the gospel to the world?

The Message of the Great Commission

Only one message has the power to change sinners and deem them righteous in Christ as a new creation. That life-transforming message is the gospel, the faith "once for all delivered to the saints" (Jude 1:3). Every Christian needs to be equipped to share the simple gospel message for the Great Commission to be fulfilled.

The message of the gospel has four main parts:

- *God loves man and desires to restore him to a personal and eternal relationship with Himself* (see John 3:16; 10:10; 2 Corinthians 5:17–18).
- *Every man is sinful and separated from God.* Without Christ man is hopelessly lost, unrighteous, alienated from God, spiritually dead in sins, enslaved to a futile way of life, under the control of Satan, destined for eternal separation from God, and totally incapable of saving himself (see Isaiah 59:1–2; John 8:34; Romans 3:23; 6:23; Ephesians 2:1–3).
- *God has graciously provided man one way of salvation through faith in His only Son, Jesus Christ.* Jesus died to pay the price for all man's sins, was buried, and rose again with power over death (see Galatians 3:6–18; Ephesians 2:8–9; Colossians 1:19–22; 1 Timothy 2:5). Jesus paid in full the price for all the sins of all men for all time.
- *God offers man a new life in Christ, but it must be received by faith.* God lovingly calls man to repent of his sins and to believe in Christ as Savior and Lord and receive the gift of forgiveness and the promise of eternal life (see John 1:12; Acts 2:38; 16:31; Romans 10:9–10; 2 Peter 3:9).

The simple message of the gospel is the power of God, wrapped up and ready to be opened by anyone willing to believe. When anyone repents and decides to place his personal faith in Jesus Christ, the Word of God declares that person to be a new creation in Christ Jesus (see 2 Corinthians 5:17), a child of God (see John 1:12), an adopted son who is sealed by the Holy Spirit and guaranteed an inheritance (see Ephesians 1:13–14; 4:30), and someone who has a prepared place in heaven (see John 14:3). A child can understand the basics of salvation, but it will take all eternity for us to fully grasp the scope and eternal ramifications of what salvation did for us.

The Gospel Message—Making Disciples

This one message of the gospel is not just about counting decisions—it's about making disciples. Christ's command is "make disciples," and that command is followed by two ways for a believer to advance in discipleship.

The first way to grow as a disciple is to be baptized: "Make disciples . . . , baptizing them in the name of the Father and of the Son and of the Holy Spirit" (Matthew 28:19). A new disciple will follow Christ's command to be baptized.

The act of baptism does not save people or wash away their sins. The Bible teaches us that baptism is the first logical step in following Christ after believing the gospel. It is the way new believers give testimony to their identity with Christ in His death, burial, and resurrection. Romans 6:4 provides the most direct teaching in the entire Bible on the theological significance of baptism: "We were buried therefore with him by baptism into death, in order that, just as Christ was raised from the dead by the glory of the Father, we too might walk in newness of life."

The whole gospel narrative is retold in baptism. When a new believer is immersed in water, it's as if he is saying, "I believe that Christ's death for sins was the death that I deserved as punishment for my sins but Christ shed His blood to free me from the awful penalty of eternal death." Then, when a new believer is raised out of the water, it's as if he is saying, "I have new life in Christ, and I believe that Christ's glorious resurrection was for me and that He has given me the promise of resurrection and everlasting life. This is a new life that I could not achieve apart from my faith in Him." While baptism today is sometimes misunderstood, understated, or ignored, it is what Jesus asked His followers to do. Jesus made baptism central to discipleship because it depicts our eternal union with Him.

While baptism is a one-time act, the second part of growing as a disciple involves one's entire life span: Jesus defined making disciples as "teaching them to observe all that I have commanded you." A disciple is a follower and a learner. Christian discipleship is the process by which disciples "grow in the grace and knowledge of our Lord and Savior Jesus Christ" (2 Peter 3:18). As the disciple grows, he overcomes the pressures and trials of this present life and becomes more Christlike in thought and behavior.

This part of the discipleship process urges believers to continually learn and respond to the Holy Spirit's prompting, examining their thoughts, words, and actions and comparing them with the Word of God. This process requires that the disciple read the Bible daily—that he study it, pray over it, and obey it. In addition, disciples should "always be prepared to give an answer to everyone who asks [them] to give the reason for the hope that [they] have" (1 Peter 3:15, NIV).

Evidences of a Disciple

Being a Christian disciple involves personal change and growth characterized by five evidences.

A disciple denies himself to follow Jesus. "Whoever does not bear his own cross and come after me cannot be my disciple" (Luke 14:27). "If anyone would come after me, let him deny himself and take up his cross daily and follow me" (Luke 9:23).

The greatest barrier to truly following Jesus as a growing disciple is preoccupation with self. The Bible plainly teaches that we have an inherently sinful nature (see Proverbs 20:9; Romans 3:23; 5:12–13; 1 John 1:8). The Bible uses other terms such as "the flesh" (Romans 7:14; 8:8; 1 Corinthians 3:3) and "old self" (Romans 6:6; Ephesians 4:22; Colossians 3:9) to describe the old nature that Christians constantly battle and must put off and put to death. This love of self will be one of the earmarks of the last days, leading to a host of other problems (see 2 Timothy 3:1–5).

By contrast, Jesus told His disciples to follow Him by denying themselves. To follow Jesus means that we, His disciples, will repudiate our own right to live the way we desire to live. We will forfeit our time, talent, and treasure for the cause of following Jesus. But in Mark 8:34-36 Jesus said that in losing our life for His sake, we actually find the best life.

A disciple consistently follows Jesus' teachings. "If you abide in my word, you are truly my disciples" (John 8:31–32). Disciples are obedient followers and doers of the Word. Obedience is the supreme test of our love for Jesus: "If you love me, you will keep my commandments" (John 14:15). Jesus defined love for Him as a quality that goes well beyond a good feeling about Him. He said that real love translates into obedience to His commands.

In His incarnation, Jesus was the perfect example of obedience. He lived a life on Earth of complete obedience to the Father, even to the point of death (see Philippians 2:6–8). Discipleship is a commitment to obey Jesus without any reluctance or reservation.

A disciple is connected to Jesus and bears fruit. "By this my Father is glorified, that you bear much fruit and so prove to be my disciples" (John 15:8). Notice that the evidence of a disciple is not *producing* fruit but *bearing* fruit. A branch cut off the vine will eventually dry up and die. Disciples are commanded to abide in Christ (see John 15:4), and when disciples abide in Christ, the Holy Spirit will produce fruit through their lives, and this fruit will bring glory to God the Father. The change Jesus desires for His disciples is done from the inside out, through the power of the Holy Spirit, as we stay connected to Jesus.

A disciple loves others as Jesus loves him. "A new commandment I give to you, that you love one another: just as I have loved you, you also are to love one another. By this all people will know that you are my disciples, if you have love for one another" (John 13:34–35). Jesus taught that love of other believers is the evidence of our being a member of God's family: "By this it is evident who are the children of God, and who are the children of the devil: whoever does not practice righteousness is not of God, nor is the one who does not love his brother" (1 John 3:10). Love is defined and elaborated on in 1 Corinthians 13. This chapter shows us that love is not an emotion; it is action. True disciples actively do something for the benefit of others.

Looking at this from another angle, we are told to think more highly of others than ourselves and to look out for their interests (see Philippians 2:3–4). The disciple who follows Jesus will increasingly live for the benefit of others, motivated by a heart of love. Philippians 2:5 sums up what a disciple's perspective ought to be: "You must have the same attitude that Christ Jesus had" (NLT). Jesus Christ is the perfect example of the loving person a disciple is intended to become.

A disciple makes disciples of others. "Go therefore and make disciples of all nations" (Matthew 28:19). Disciples are commanded to share their faith in Christ. Disciples can tell nonbelievers about the wonderful changes that Jesus Christ has made in their lives.

Our Lord has commissioned each of us to share the gospel and "seek the lost." He said, "Go therefore and make disciples of all nations" (Matthew 28:19), and, "Go into all the world and proclaim the gospel to the whole creation" (Mark 16:15). The disciple's greatest calling is to share the new life that Jesus has given him with those who have not received Christ as their Savior and Lord.

New disciples need not wait to share their faith with others. Some of the most enthusiastic representatives of the Christian life are new believers who have just discovered the awesome love of God. They may not know all the necessary Bible verses or the best way to say things, but they have experienced the love of the living God, and that is exactly what disciples are to share.

Think It Over: The Message of the Great Commission

1. If you were asked to lead someone to faith in Jesus Christ, what would you say? How would you lead the person step by step?
2. Why did Jesus say to "make disciples" rather than to "record decisions"?
3. What are the marks of a disciple?
4. Which one of the marks of discipleship do you need to most work on? Why?
5. Why should anyone listen to you present the gospel?

The Messengers of the Great Commission

God has not only ordained the motivation, means, and message of the gospel, but He has also ordained the messengers who are to take the message of the gospel into the world: His people. Several times as I heard the late missionary statesman Dr. Dick Hillis preach, he made this easy to understand: "Everyone with Christ is a missionary; everyone without Christ is a mission field."

While methods and cultural adaptations may vary from culture to culture, the messengers of the gospel generally present the good news in two ways: proclamation evangelism and personal evangelism.

Proclamation Evangelism

Proclamation evangelism involves a large gathering of people with an evangelist preaching. Proclamation evangelistic events are usually well organized, publicized in advance, and meant to declare the gospel to the masses.

Acts 13:43–44 relates an example of mass evangelism. In Antioch of Pisidia, Paul and Barnabas drew large crowds of both Jews and Gentiles, who listened with great interest. The Bible says that "almost the whole city gathered to hear the word of the Lord" (Acts 13:44). The Word of God spread from Antioch to the surrounding region as Gentiles enthusiastically believed in Christ.

Some of the Jews in Antioch, however, stirred up persecution and drove Paul and Barnabas out of the region. This points out some of the advantages and drawbacks of proclamation evangelism.

Advantages of Proclamation	Disadvantages of Proclamation
Draws attention to Christ	Draws undesirable pubic attention
Creates buzz	Stirs up adversaries
Requires a gifted evangelist	Relies on one main preacher
Brings like-minded Christians together	Makes it difficult to keep track of decisions
Pools resources	Provides no opportunity to build relationships
Is organized	Makes it difficult to follow up on decisions

Proclamation evangelism is a biblical method of reaching the lost that has its advantages and disadvantages. There is a time and place for a bold and public declaration of the gospel to the masses. Given the organizational requirements of a large event, it takes a well-built infrastructure to carry out this method of evangelism.

As a method of carrying out the Great Commission, proclamation evangelism has a lower statistical outcome than personal evangelism does. For that reason, the emphasis in the church should be on personal evangelism.

Personal Evangelism

Personal evangelism, also called friendship or lifestyle evangelism, is not an event but a way of thinking. It is a method of evangelism that every Christian can do. Every believer has relationships with unbelievers, so the genius of personal evangelism is that it connects believers with unbelievers in the context of friendship.

Personal evangelism naturally relies on the relationships that Christians develop on the job, in school, around the neighborhood, at civic organizations, at sporting events, and in business. The goal is to build relationships with unbelievers in which trust is gained and the opportunity to share Christ becomes natural. The gospel is presented personally and even privately in the context of a growing relationship.

Personal evangelism has some distinct advantages. It gives the message credibility, and it provides the recipient the opportunity to ponder and ask questions. The call to make a decision for Christ is not as uncomfortable in the personal setting as it is in a public event.

But personal evangelism has some disadvantages over proclamation evangelism. Personal evangelism requires time in which to build relationships, and it relies on believers to consistently live out their faith in public without becoming annoying preachy Christians. That means showing care, concern, and practical help to others. When unbelievers experience a believer who loves them, the barriers that often stand in the way of considering the message of Christ seem to crumble. Love crosses all emotional, intellectual, and cultural boundaries.

One benefit of personal evangelism is that it is easy to follow up on people saved in this way. The percentage of people who make decisions at public events who actually connect to a local church where they can grow and be discipled is low. When personal evangelism is the approach, on the other hand, the percentage of those who ultimately connect with a local church skyrockets. Friendship evangelism is proven to be the most successful method because it is built on trusted relationships. It more easily bridges cultural gaps, and it offers the best way to disciple new believers and integrate them into a local church.

The advantages and disadvantages of personal evangelism can be seen in the chart on the next page.

Think It Over: The Messengers of the Great Commission

1. What are the two basic ways the gospel is shared?
2. In which of these ways do you feel most experienced?

Advantages of Personal Evangelism	Disadvantages of Personal Evangelism
Relies on every believer's obedience	Relies on every believer being willing to share
Allows friendship to open the door	Depends on Christians to faithfully live the Christian life
Builds trust naturally	Risks a relationship if the gospel is rejected
Calls every Christian to share testimony	Depends on every Christian to prepare
Happens over time	Takes longer for people to make a decision
Leaves room for questions	Requires Christian to be ready with answers
Allows the call for decision to be private	Can make the call for a decision awkward
Makes follow-up natural	Requires a time commitment for follow-up

3. What are the pros and cons of proclamation evangelism?
4. Why do you think that personal evangelism is statistically the most effective way to lead someone to Christ?
5. What additional training or motivating do you need to be a better personal evangelist?
6. What evangelism training can you give to others?
7. Which unsaved people in your family, job, or neighborhood would you like to personally share Christ with?
8. When will you start?

The Map of the Great Commission

The Bible commands us to reach the entire world with the gospel. Earlier in this chapter we saw five passages in Scripture in which Jesus gave the Great Commission. In each of these passages we see the "map," or the extent of the area, that shows where we are to take the gospel:

Scripture	Recipients
Matthew 28:18–20	"All nations"
Mark 16:15,19–22	"The whole creation"
Luke 24:46–49	"All nations, beginning from Jerusalem"
John 17:18; 20:21–23	"The world" (which hates believers)
Acts 1:8	"Jerusalem and in all Judea and Samaria, and to the end of the earth"

Upon closer examination of Jesus' commands, we find that Acts 1:8 gives us specifics on what the map looks like. In this verse Jesus gave us both a geographical progression and a cultural progression in advancing the gospel into the entire world.

The Geographical Progression

The geographical progression in Acts 1:8 begins where the disciples were living at the time when Jesus gave them the map: Jerusalem. Jesus commanded His disciples to take the gospel out like waves spread from a pebble thrown into a pond, beginning with Jerusalem—the geographical heart and center of Jewish religious and cultural life. Each concentric circle advanced the gospel to the next logical geographical location. Jerusalem was the capital, Judea was the surrounding area, Samaria was more than a day's journey away, and the end of the earth covered the rest of the world. Why is this significant?

Historically speaking, the book of Acts recounts this exact geographical progression. Acts 1–7 tell of the first Christians, who were Jews living in Jerusalem. Acts 8–12 tell of the gospel advancing to Judea and Samaria. Acts 13–28 record the advance of the gospel into the wider expanse of the Roman Empire. By application, the plan that Jesus gave His disciples is the same for every believer and every church. The witness of the church should start in the geographical neighborhood around them. Then it should continue in successive order to the next logical locations in ever-expanding circles, until the end of the earth is reached. In the twenty-first century, with the use of new technologies and possibilities for speedy travel, every Christian leader and every church should think about using the entire map that Jesus gave, from local to global.

The Cultural Progression

The Great Commission map that Jesus gave to His disciples in Acts 1:8 was intended to cross cultural boundaries. Jesus came for the whole world, not just for the Jews who were from His cultural, religious, and geographical context. Jesus said, "I have other sheep that are not of this fold. I must bring them also, and they will listen to my voice. So there will be one flock, one shepherd" (John 10:16). God's plan has always been to provide Jesus as the Savior for the whole world (see Luke 2:30–32; John 3:16).

The advance of the gospel into cultures and nations beyond Israel is well documented in Acts. Advancing the gospel across cultural lines was a big struggle for the early church. God used Phillip to break the cultural and ethnic barrier when he traveled to Samaria and preached to the Samarians (see Acts 8:4–25). Most Jews despised Samaritans. The Samaritans were the mixed-race descendants of the Jews who had been left in Israel when the Babylonian king, Nebuchadnezzar, had conquered Judah in 587 BC. The cultural animosity between Jews and Samaritans had historical roots that went deep.

When Phillip preached the gospel in Samaria, the message of Jesus was enthusiastically received (see Acts 8:4–8). Hearing of the gospel's cultural advance, the apostles in Jerusalem sent Peter and John to Samaria to investigate (see Acts 8:14), and God confirmed to them His intent for the gospel to cross into the Samaritan culture with the powerful evidence of the Holy Spirit being given to the new believers (see Acts 8:17). Peter and John quickly adapted to the gospel's advance into a cousin culture: "When they had testified and spoken the word of the Lord, they returned to Jerusalem, preaching the gospel to many villages of the Samaritans" (Acts 8:25).

The next advance of the gospel came to a culture and ethnicity outside the context of Israel. Once again God used Philip to bring the message of the gospel:

> An angel of the Lord said to Philip, "Rise and go toward the south to the road that goes down from Jerusalem to Gaza." This is a desert place. And he rose and went. And there was an Ethiopian, a eunuch,

> a court official of Candace, queen of the Ethiopians, who was in charge of all her treasure. He had come to Jerusalem to worship and was returning, seated in his chariot, and he was reading the prophet Isaiah. And the Spirit said to Philip, "Go over and join this chariot." (Acts 8:26–29)

The story of the Ethiopian eunuch from the royal court of Candace clearly shows the intention of God to advance the gospel beyond the cultural and ethnic boundaries familiar to the first disciples. The Ethiopians had a long history with Israel dating back to the time of King Solomon, but they had their own distinct culture. Phillip is sometimes lost in the story of the advance of the gospel because of the powerful presence of Peter or Paul. However, Phillip was God's first ambassador to the cultural world outside the holy land. God miraculously intervened and broke the cultural and racial barrier into the rest of the world with the conversion of the Ethiopian eunuch on the road to Gaza, making this man the first non-Jew to receive the gospel.

Another huge cultural advance for the gospel came when Cornelius, a Roman centurion, received a vision to go and seek out the apostle Peter, who was residing at Simon the tanner's house in Joppa. What made this advance so significant was the cultural and political distance between the Jews and their Roman oppressors. The Romans were a cruel occupying force. They had carried out the crucifixion of Jesus under Pontius Pilate. So for God to give a vision to a Roman centurion was astonishing to the early Jewish believers. There was so much animosity and cultural distance between Jews and Romans that God had to use a dramatic vision to speak to Peter about His intent to take the gospel to the Gentiles:

> There came a voice to him: "Rise, Peter; kill and eat." But Peter said, "By no means, Lord; for I have never eaten anything that is common or unclean." And the voice came to him again a second time, "What God has made clean, do not call common." This happened three times, and the thing was taken up at once to heaven. (Acts 10:13–16)

Crossing this religious, emotional, and political boundary had to be immensely difficult for Peter, for three reasons. First, Peter was a proper

Jew, and Cornelius was a Gentile. Jews had little to do with Gentiles. Second, Cornelius was a Roman, and Peter had personally witnessed the Roman soldiers brutally beat and then crucify Jesus. This fearful memory of Roman behavior would have been an emotional barrier for Peter. Third, Rome was an occupying military force in Israel. This raised strong political objections by Jews living in first-century Israel. So God used a dramatic vision to call Peter to take the gospel well beyond his religious, emotional, and political boundaries. It is not surprising that God had to give Peter this vision three times before he was willing to listen and obey. But because Peter obeyed and went, Cornelius, the Roman military officer, was the first Gentile of the Roman world to hear the gospel and believe in Jesus. From this time onward, the gospel was taken to the ends of the earth.

How does this relate to the church today? If the church in the twenty-first century is to fulfill the Great Commission, it will need to expand its geographical reach and move outside its ethnic, political, and cultural boundaries. Geographically, every church must begin by sharing the gospel within their immediate locale. Then it must intentionally move beyond its immediate area into the region, the country, and even the world! In such a scenario, partnerships with other mission organizations and churches are more easily forged and more productive than ever before.

Much like the first-century church, our biggest difficulty in advancing the gospel today is not geographical but cultural. Crossing cultural, ethnic, tribal, religious, political, and linguistic barriers remains a challenge for the church. This is where the church needs a new vision from the Lord and new obedience to reach beyond.

Normally those who come from the same cultural context as the intended receptors of the message will be more effective at communicating in a culturally relevant manner than those from another cultural context. In some situations, however, there are not yet enough evangelists and disciple makers available from the local cultural context to effectively reach everyone. In these situations the most effective evangelists and disciple makers will usually be those who best adapt to the cultural context.

In general, missionary theorists and practitioners have long seen effective cultural contextualization as one of the most important factors affecting the ultimate success of fulfilling the Great Commission. However, crossing the barriers requires hard, diligent effort on the part of the missionary. In spite of the progress that has been made by diligent efforts toward cultural contextualization on the part of missionary workers, the best ongoing solution for the advance of the gospel is to transfer the main responsibility of communicating the gospel to those who come from the same cultural context as those in need of the gospel as much as possible and as soon as possible.

Principle of Building Bridges Across Cultural Divides

In order to achieve God's purpose of getting the message of the gospel to the lost, God's messengers will have to adapt their methods to each place they go. This will be necessary because each group they minister to will receive the message in different ways.

When the apostle Paul preached the gospel throughout the ancient Roman Empire and encountered various cultures and people groups, his listeners responded differently in each place he went. In Berea he found Jews who were "more noble than those in Thessalonica" (Acts 17:11), for these Berean Jews examined the Scriptures carefully to see if what Paul was preaching fit the prophetic record in the Old Testament. The Bereans were traditional religious Jews whose source of religious authority was Scripture.

In the neighboring city of Thessalonica, Paul encountered a culturally different kind of people than he had at Berea. The Hellenists were not culturally religious. We would refer to them as secularists who had adapted to the prevailing Greco-Roman culture. When Paul preached at Thessalonica, some of the Hellenistic Greeks and Jews accepted his message about Jesus, while others gathered a mob and used violence and false accusation to stop Paul from preaching.

Later in Acts 17 we find Paul preaching in the ancient city of Athens, which was yet another cultural context. As the intellectual center of the ancient world, Athens prided itself as an open-minded symposium in which new ideas could be presented for debate and evaluation.

Because of the differences between these three cities, while Paul's message about Christ did not change, his manner of presentation did. In Thessalonica Paul spent three days in the synagogue reasoning from the Scriptures to overcome the skepticism of the Jews and Greeks. His approach in Thessalonica was an apologetic one supported by Scripture in order to prove that Jesus was the Messiah. In the city of Berea, because the townsfolk were eager to receive the gospel message, Paul presented to them evidence from the Old Testament about Jesus as the Messiah. Many in Berea believed because they were ready to consider this evidence from Scripture. For the intellectual elite of Athens, Paul's evangelistic approach took an abrupt turn, since the Athenians did not view the Hebrew Scriptures as authoritative. In Athens Paul's preaching appealed to logic, literature, history, philosophy, and religion. Paul's presentation of the gospel of Jesus Christ was brilliantly done, but it was in such stark contrast to the religions and philosophies of the Athenians that it appears that no one in Athens believed in Jesus.

The principle of cultural adaptation is articulated in 1 Corinthians 9:19–23:

> Though I am free from all, I have made myself a servant to all, that I might win more of them. To the Jews I became as a Jew, in order to win Jews. To those under the law I became as one under the law (though not being myself under the law) that I might win those under the law. To those outside the law I became as one outside the law (not being outside the law of God but under the law of Christ) that I might win those outside the law. To the weak I became weak, that I might win the weak. I have become all things to all people, that by all means I might save some. I do it all for the sake of the gospel, that I may share with them in its blessings.

Think It Over: The Map of the Great Commission

1. Why did Jesus ask His disciples to begin reaching the world starting with their current location?
2. Where do you think God would like you to start witnessing?
3. Name the geographical and cultural areas surrounding you that correspond to those in Acts 1:8.
4. What barriers exist in your life, leadership, and church that prevent the fulfillment of the Great Commission? What can you do about them?

5. What philosophical, ideological, social, or political barriers challenge the spread of the gospel around you? What response will you make regarding them?

Barriers in the Church to Fulfilling the Great Commission

If geographical and cultural barriers were instantly removed, we would still find barriers inside some churches to prevent the fulfillment of the Great Commission. Every church leader and pastor needs to look deep into the self-imposed barriers that keep a church from answering the command of Christ to make disciples.

Lack of pastoral leadership is likely the biggest barrier to advancing the gospel beyond the local church. A pastor without a passion for the lost is a roadblock to his church. Pastors are often so busy putting out fires in their own congregation that they have little time to think of anyone beyond their church. There will never be a time when it is convenient or easy to advance the gospel. Pastors must stretch themselves and commit to leading their congregation in missions.

Lack of vision is another barrier that keeps churches from impacting the world for Jesus Christ. Sometimes church leaders can be so overwhelmed by the size of the task that they give up before starting. A missions vision should be big enough to challenge the church but small enough to be able to accomplish. Missions vision is something that should be prayed for and acted on as the Lord speaks. When my church, Cornerstone Church, began as a small group, we did not know if we could afford a pastor's salary as well as overhead. But we made a commitment to give 20 percent to missions. God honored that commitment, and today Cornerstone has a large missions vision.

Lack of evangelistic training keeps most churches from mobilizing their people. In the average lifetime of a Christian in America, most do not share their faith and see someone come to know Christ. That is a shocking but true statistic. Because of a lack of training, the job of evangelism has been relegated to the "professional" pastors or evangelists. To remove this barrier, every church must take the matter of evangelistic training seriously. Friendship evangelism is the most natural and effective method.

Philosophical Barriers	Biblical Answer
Humanism, atheism. There is no God, so man is his own god and the measure of all things.	There is only one eternal God, who has revealed Himself in His only Son, Jesus Christ. Man is finite and has proven throughout history to be incapable of governing himself. Man is the creation of God, made in God's image but fallen in sin (see Psalm 8:1–9; Hebrews 1:1–2).
Materialism. There is nothing beyond the material universe. The goal of life is to get as much as one can.	Materialism cannot account for man's universal quest for love, justice, or God. More material things do not satisfy the deep longings of man for purpose (see Luke 12:13–21).
Hedonism. The quest for pleasure is life's goal.	Pleasure is temporary and diminishes with time. The quest for pleasure turns to despair (see Ecclesiastes 2:1–11; Hebrews 11:24–26).
Existentialism. Life is what you make it to be. Existence precedes essence.	Man exists as the creation of God and has a limited freedom to choose within God's sovereign and limitless authority (see Psalm 8:1–9; Romans 11:33–36).
Religious Barriers	**Biblical Answer**
Pantheism. All is God, and God is all.	God is infinitely greater than the entire universe. He exists above and beyond His creation (transcendently) but works within it (imminently) to do His will (see Genesis 1:1; Psalm 33:1–15).
Polytheism. There are many gods. Polytheists consider Jesus to be only one of many gods in this world.	The gods of this world are dead, powerless, and worthless. There is only one true God who exists in three equal and eternal persons: Father, Son, and Holy Spirit (see Isaiah 44:6–20; Matthew 28:19).
Syncretism. There are many roads to heaven. All religions worship God under a different name.	Jesus claimed to be the only way to God. When compared to Christianity, other religious teachings have irreconcilable conflicts (see John 14:6; 2 Corinthians 6:14–18).

Religious Barriers (*Continued*)	**Biblical Answer** (*Continued*)
Universalism. All humanity will be saved, regardless of religion or belief system.	Only those who believe in Jesus Christ as Savior will be saved (see John 6:40; 14:6; Romans 10:9–10).
Animism. Natural objects and phenomena possess spirits and have spiritual power.	God exists outside of the natural objects and animals that He created. His eternal power and divine nature are revealed in what He created. He is Spirit and is uniquely distinct from and infinitely greater than what He has created (see 1 Kings 8:27; Psalm 19:1–6; John 1:1–2; 4:24; Acts 17:24; Romans 1:19–20).
Islam. Allah is God, Mohammed is his prophet, and the Koran is his book. Both good and evil come from Allah and are his will. Heaven is a male-dominated paradise of sensual desire. The duty of man is to surrender to the will of Allah and obey the five pillars of Islam.	There is only one true God who exists in three coequal and coeternal persons, Father, Son, and Holy Spirit. He is holy and never evil. Jesus Christ is God the Son. He is the crucified and risen Savior of the world. Forgiveness of sins and eternal life are found only in Him. The Bible is the inspired and inerrant revelation of God (see Isaiah 6:1–3; 44:6–8; 1 Timothy 2:5; 2 Timothy 3:16).
Hinduism. There are thousands of Hindu gods. All living beings come from the same origin. Man can transcend consciousness and be integrated into the one transcendent source. The laws of Karma and reincarnation dictate all of life.	There is only one true God. God created man and desires to have fellowship with us. Jesus took all sin upon Himself and died to pay sin's penalty so that we can be free from judgment for our sins (see Genesis 2–3; Romans 6:23; 1 John 1:9).
Buddhism. There is no god. Buddha never claimed to be god. Life is a riddle. Man seeks the path of enlightenment through self-denial. Nirvana is a passionless state of blissful oblivion.	There is one personal God who eternally exists. The object of life is to know Him personally through His only Son, Jesus Christ, and to glorify Him forever (see Isaiah 44:6–8; John 17:3).

Religious Barriers (*Continued*)	Biblical Answer (*Continued*)
Christian liberalism. Jesus is not God and did not rise from the dead. The Bible contains myths and is best used as a book of ethics. Mankind's greatest need is social change, not redemption through faith in Jesus Christ.	Jesus is God, and His resurrection is a fact of history recorded in the Bible and in other sources. The Bible is inerrant and has been proven true in every detail. Every man needs redemption. The duty of Christians is to fulfill the Great Commission and to love their neighbor (see Matthew 24:35; 28:19–20; John 1:1, 12; 1 Corinthians 15).

Political Barriers	Biblical Answer
Nationalism. Nations exist independently and have no need of God. Nations are accountable only to themselves. Allegiance to one's nation is more important than to God.	God is sovereign and in control over the nations. One day Jesus will judge all nations (see Psalm 117:1–2; Daniel 2:20–23; Joel 3:12; Matthew 25; Revelation 20:11–15).
Communism. There is no god; the state is god. The political system controls everything and everyone for the good of the state.	Only a fool says that there is no god. Creation and everything in it belongs to God, not the state. The duty of government is to keep order and avenge the wrongdoer. Governments rise and fall by God's authority (see Psalm 14:1; 24:1; Proverbs 21:1; John 1:1–2; Romans 13:1–7).
Liberation theology. The ultimate goal of life is to free the people of the world from economic, political, and social oppression.	God's ultimate desire is that all people be saved through faith in Jesus and be with Him forever in heaven. Human justice and mercy are the outgrowth of reverence for God (see Micah 6:8; John 14:1–3; 2 Peter 3:9).

Lack of boldness prevents believers from sharing their faith. Fear of rejection or of not knowing enough to share effectively contributes to a lack of boldness. However, the most basic reason for a lack of boldness is the absence of the filling of the Holy Spirit. Watch a new believer share enthusiastically, and it becomes evident that he has no fear, only freedom.

Lack of planning stops many churches from advancing the gospel. If a church's goal is nothing, it will be sure to hit it every time. Advance planning to reach out with the gospel marshals a church's resources and focuses people's hearts on the objective of reaching the lost.

Lack of financial resources is an excuse that some churches use to justify their non-involvement in the Great Commission. When a church steps out in faith to obey Christ's command, they will receive Christ's blessing. God's work done in God's way for God's glory will never lack for God's resources. The decision Cornerstone Church made to sacrificially give to local and global missions was the best decision we made in the early days. As we sacrificed to get the gospel out beyond our doors, God grew and enriched our church beyond measure. It is a matter of faith, not finances.

But barriers to the Great Commission are found not only in the church. The world is filled with competing ideologies and compelling messages that hinder the spread of the gospel. Major philosophical, religious, and ideological barriers to the spread of the gospel exist, but for each of them, we find a counter argument from the Bible. The chart beginning on page 161 details these.

Think It Over: Barriers in the Church to Fulfilling the Great Commission

1. How would you rate the negative impact in your church of the six main barriers that keep churches from sharing the gospel?
2. What are the biggest philosophical, religious, and political barriers in the neighborhood surrounding your church?
3. What goals will you set to address these barriers with prayer, training, education, motivation, and resources?

CONCLUSION:
The Pastoral Leader and the Great Commission

The future of the world awaits the obedience of the church to the Great Commission. The parade of empty philosophies, false religions, and oppressive political ideologies will continue to lure and deceive. But we know that God is a God of infinite love and grace, and He is not willing that any should perish but that all should come to repentance (see 2 Peter 3:9). God's world is waiting for the strategic and Spirit-directed proclamation of the gospel.

I believe that this is the message that Jesus has for the church today: "Do you not say, 'There are yet four months, then comes the harvest'? Look, I tell you, lift up your eyes, and see that the fields are white for harvest" (John 4:35).

8

The Pastoral Leader and Counseling

Objective: *To provide a plan for pastors to administer pastoral care and counseling to their flock and community.*

Given the pastor's role as a spiritual leader and caregiver to the flock, the pastor is often the first person people go to for help. In medical terminology the pastor is the emergency triage resource who is first on the scene of suffering, misunderstanding, or tragedy.

Emergency medical professionals are trained in emergency life-sustaining procedures, but the average pastor has very little training in caring for the wounded of his flock. This puts the pastor in an awkward position in which he is expected to know what to do but has never been given training on how to do it. This chapter is not designed to give a pastor all the necessary training and resources that he will need to be an effective counselor—achieving that takes years of school and experience. The goal of this chapter is to provide pastors with a basic approach to counseling.

Pastoral counseling is fundamentally the application of the work of Christ to a wide range of human brokenness. The vast array of people's weakness, frailty, imperfection, injustice, abuse, and evil calls for the application of Christ's love, care, and healing.

From the book of Job, the archetype of suffering, comes this truth: "Man is born to trouble as the sparks fly upward" (Job 5:7). The Bible confirms that everyone is commonly exposed to a wide variety of troubles, as if they were born for trouble without a choice. Affliction, pain, confusion, and loss are natural to fallen man living in a fallen world. Problems can originate from internal struggles, issues transmitted from parents to children, broken relationships, death or loss, demonic activity, physical or mental illness, and a wide variety of other circumstances that we encounter in our sinful world. Troubles come naturally, and as universally, "as the sparks" of fire "fly upward." Why then should we be surprised at our afflictions and think of them as strangers or quarrel with them as enemies?

James 1:2–5 gives us a biblical perspective on how to approach the challenges and problems of this life:

> Count it all joy, my brothers, when you meet trials of various kinds, for you know that the testing of your faith produces steadfastness. And let steadfastness have its full effect, that you may be perfect and complete, lacking in nothing.
>
> If any of you lacks wisdom, let him ask God, who gives generously to all without reproach, and it will be given him.

Pastoral counseling is designed to help a believer think biblically, feel hopeful, and act wisely while going through the struggles and challenges of life. Pastoral counseling makes use of the Word of God to bring about change in the person's thinking, feeling, and actions and to help him grasp the abundant life that Christ promised (see John 10:10).

Every pastor needs a basic framework or biblical philosophy for the ministry of counseling. The book of James gives six helpful principles to believers who face agonizing trials; these same principles act as a guide for pastors who administer compassion and help people through pastoral counseling. I've used this basic counseling framework for many years with success. Learning this approach has two advantages: first, it gives the pastor a biblical framework to guide him; second, it will save the pastor many hours of wasted time in assessment, therapy, and follow-up.

Approach Problems with a Positive Attitude

The first piece of advice James gives that helps us form a framework for biblical counseling is to approach every problem with a positive attitude: "Count it all joy, my brothers, when you meet trials of various kinds" (James 1:2).

The greatest predictor of whether a counselee will be open to resolution and healing for the presenting problem is the attitude he takes with him going into treatment. The lame man lying beside the Pool of Bethesda teaches a powerful lesson regarding the first step in healing and paralyzing trial: "When Jesus saw him lying there and knew that he had already been there a long time, he said to him, 'Do you want to be healed?'" (John 5:5-6). The lame man had been there so long and suffered so much that he no longer believed that his circumstance could change. This illustrates the first principle in counseling: people do not get well until they *want* to get well.

An emotionally sick person can actually attach his identity to his suffering so that he cannot see himself apart from his problem. A deeply hurt or angry person may not be ready to resolve his hurt or forgive those who have sinned against him. His pain makes him "feel good" because it calls others to feel sympathy for him; meanwhile, he makes excuses for himself so that he can stay in the pain and not get well. Counselees have thousands of reasons why they feel justified in hanging on to their hurt and pain.

One of the first things a pastor must learn about a counselee is whether the person has the desire to make necessary changes and the willpower and faith to be healed. This sounds almost too elementary, but from years of practice, I have learned to look for the counselee's motivation to get well. Unmotivated counselees are like people who go to the doctor with a painful boil. They do not want it lanced and cleaned out; they merely want the doctor to offer sympathy and give them temporary pain relief. Unless the person has a desire to be healed, the pastor and the counselee are wasting time.

James wrote his letter to Christians who were suffering for their faith—people who had suffered the loss of every material possession and who lived in daily insecurity. James counseled them this way: "Count it all joy, my brothers, when you meet trials of various kinds." A paraphrase of this verse could sound like this: "If you cannot change your bad situation, change your attitude about it." James is not recommending a martyr complex, as if someone in a struggle is supposed to be happy about the pain he is suffering. Pain and suffering are not joyful. James is offering a fresh perspective and a workable tactic for facing troubles. He is counseling persecuted Christians to "count it all joy" because God always has good reasons behind the struggles we face—because suffering is God's way of bringing personal maturity, growth, and blessing. Romans 8:28 is either a dangerous and false statement, or it is the most hopeful verse in the Bible for suffering Christians: "We know that for those who love God all things work together for good, for those who are called according to his purpose."

The first step in getting well is for a person to choose a hopeful perspective that changes his present attitude and his future direction. What is that transforming perspective? That God is using the troubling issues of our lives to bring about higher purposes in us! That's reason to rejoice.

Think It Over: Approach Problems with a Positive Attitude

1. What is the first thing you must learn about a person who has come to you for counseling?
2. What is God's purpose in the trials people experience?
3. How can you help someone in need of counseling to "count it all joy" in the midst of trial? What Scriptures could you point the person to?

Approach Problems as Tests of Faith

The second principle of biblical counseling is to approach every problem understanding that trials are fundamentally a test of faith in God: "You know that the testing of your faith produces steadfastness" (James 1:3).

Whether the presenting problem is depression, financial worry, or marital tension, it will cause the counselee's trust in God and in God's Word to be tested. The Word of God has much to say about such things as anxiety, depression, fear, jealousy, anger, sexual sin, marital failure, frustration, and resentment. In almost every instance these problems involve some kind of sinful behavior that is connected to some unwise, untrue, or ungodly thinking. And what we think and believe controls our feelings and behaviors.

For instance, if you were sitting in a room with me and I lied to you and told you that the building was on fire, how would you feel? If you truly believed me, you would feel fear for your life. And what action would you take? Most likely you would run out of the building to safety. One could say that your feelings and action were justified and normal because you thought the building was on fire—yet your feelings and actions would have been based on a lie!

Likewise, people who are dealing with depression, anxiety, resentment, or any other dark issue are also dealing with wrong thinking in one form or another. In light of that fact, three basic factors must be in place for counselees to move toward emotional health and healing: First, counselees must know the truth about what the Bible teaches regarding human struggles like fear, failure, depression, divorce, suicide, and many others. Second, counselees must know the truth that God truly loves, cares, and understands them. Third, counselees must believe the truth that God is completely faithful to the promises in His Word. These three building blocks of faith stand behind all healing.

When tragedy causes a believer to feel worried, anxious, fearful, angry, and out of control, his emotions are fueled by negative thoughts and unbelief. In such anxious moments the counselee cannot see that God can forgive the past, heal the present, and direct the future. Yet God says, "I will instruct you and teach you in the way you should go; I will counsel you with my eye upon you" (Psalm 32:8). How does God counsel us in the way we should go? Through the truth of His Word, which counteracts our faulty thinking.

For example, a depressed believer who feels rejected, unloved, inadequate, and worthless most likely does not believe that God loves him without condition. Yet God says, "I have loved you with an everlasting love; therefore I have continued my faithfulness to you" (Jeremiah 31:3). The jealous person is troubled with selfishness and a sense of entitlement and does not trust God to provide. But God promises every believer, "God will supply every need of yours according to his riches in glory in Christ Jesus" (Philippians 4:19). The person who has suffered abuse at the hands of others needs to know that God has not abandoned him on his long road to healing: "Fear not, for I have redeemed you; I have called you by name, you are mine. When you pass through the waters, I will be with you; and through the rivers, they shall not overwhelm you; when you walk through fire you shall not be burned, and the flame shall not consume you" (Isaiah 43:1–2).

Some believers get angry or bitter because they selfishly and irrationally believe that everything ought to go their way. When their plans are thwarted or they are offended, they respond in anger. A biblical counselor knows that at the foundation of anger are typically hurt and a lack of forgiveness. In all pastoral counseling an underlying spiritual issue relates to the believer's faith.

When someone is confused, wounded, or angry, and a pastor shows sympathy and offers counsel, he must do so without undermining the person's faith. A pastor's sympathy and counsel are not excuses for a counselee to feel self-pity but motivations to build the person's courage and fortify his faith. Healing comes when a wounded person's confidence in God grows.

Think It Over: Approach Problems as Tests of Faith

1. What is typically at the root of people's depression, fear, anxiety, or other problem?
2. How can you help people turn from wrong thinking to the truth of God's Word in a way that is kind and sympathetic?

Approach Problems with Steadfastness

Third, James encourages us to approach every problem with steadfastness: "Let steadfastness have its full effect" (James 1:4).

"I tried what you said, but it didn't work." Every pastor has heard this sad and defeated refrain from someone who came to him for help and was given biblically based counsel but then returned discouraged and disillusioned. But both counselors and counselees must honestly admit the fact that most healing comes in stages, just as most troubles develop over a period of time. Instantaneous and miraculous healing is always possible with God, but most issues require time and perseverance to resolve.

The Bible tells the story of Naaman, the commanding general of Syria's armies in the days of the prophet Elisha. Naaman had leprosy, an incurable disease at that time, and he came to the prophet for help. Elisha's instructions were not what Naaman had expected. Elisha sent his servant to Naaman to tell him, "'Go and wash in the Jordan seven times, and your flesh shall be restored, and you shall be clean.' But Naaman was angry and went away, saying, 'Behold, I thought that he would surely come out to me and stand and call upon the name of the Lord his God, and wave his hand over the place and cure the leper'" (2 Kings 5:10–11).

Oftentimes a pastor gives godly counsel only to have the person seeking advice walk out angry or disappointed. Why does this happen? First, because pastors are not infallible—this is why the counsel a pastor gives must be always thought through carefully and given prayerfully. I wish I could say that everyone who has received godly counsel from me has taken it cheerfully and used it successfully. Second, because people who come for counseling often expect the pastor to say what they want to hear. When he does not, they go away disgusted and angry.

The story of Naaman illustrates how godly but unexpected counsel does not need to end in frustration if the counselee is willing to trust the counsel, obey it, and persevere. Naaman's story points the way: "His servants came near and said to him, 'My father, it is a great word the prophet has spoken to you; will you not do it? Has he actually said to you, "Wash, and be clean"?' So he went down and dipped himself seven times in the Jordan, according to the word of the man of God, and his flesh was restored like the flesh of a little child, and he was clean" (2 Kings 5:13–14).

What would have happened if Naaman had not reconsidered his response after his initial disappointment? With a dreaded disease like leprosy, Naaman would have suffered the rest of his life and then died a slow and painful death. In the same manner, when godly counsel is rejected, people get angry (quietly or loudly) and never find healing. In addition, people who partially obey godly counsel or quit obeying after a short time will find themselves disappointed and even disillusioned.

Healing comes when a wounded person continues believing, thinking, and acting in a manner consistent with godly counsel. Some issues take longer than others to resolve. Patience and perseverance are the nurses that administer healing to broken spirits, minds, emotions, and wills in God's rehabilitation hospital. James's words ring true: "Let steadfastness have its full effect."

Think It Over: Approach Problems with Steadfastness

1. How do you answer a person who has received godly counsel from you but comes back to you feeling as if the counsel didn't work? How can your steadfastness in God's Word help the person become spiritually steadfast as well?

2. How should you respond when someone you have counseled leaves angry or disgusted?

Approach Problems with a Desire to Grow Through Them

The fourth principle from James that applies to biblical counseling is to approach every problem with a desire to grow through it. When a person does this, he will "be perfect and complete, lacking in nothing" (James 1:4).

My grandfather was a farmer in the American Midwest, where it was hard to grow crops and make enough to live. He worked hard every year planting, cultivating, and tending the crops, yet some years his yield was small, other years he had bumper crops, and a few years the crops failed altogether and produced nothing. Farmers need to be patient people, because times of rapid growth are uncertain. So it is with working through difficult emotional and relationship issues. They take time and a commitment to keep growing.

Growth means change, and change is difficult for people, because we are creatures of habit. For someone who has struggled with anger or anxiety or lust for years, it will take continuous effort and support to establish new patterns of thinking and behavior. People who have deeply ingrained habits of thinking and behavior need the additional help of structure and accountability to maintain their advances in growth. On a practical level that could mean changes in schedules, activities, boundaries, and the benefit of an accountability support group to address their issue with others who have the same struggle. Many churches have support groups that meet weekly to address issues like addiction, grief, abortion, sexual abuse, anger, and more.

Growth is a lifetime plan for every child of God. To remain stuck in a state of immaturity is not necessary or normal for the Christian, as the writer of Hebrews made clear: "Though by this time you ought to be teachers, you need someone to teach you again the basic principles of the oracles of God" (Hebrews 5:12). God's plan is for us to keep making forward progress without stopping or getting stuck.

Think It Over: Approach Problems with a Desire to Grow Through Them

1. What are some ways you can cultivate an attitude of patient growth in your congregation and in the people you counsel?
2. What support groups do you need or do you already have in your church to address the aftercare of counselees?

Approach Problems Asking God for Wisdom

The fifth piece of advice from James that we can apply to wise counseling is to approach every problem asking God for wisdom to solve it: "If any of you lacks wisdom, let him ask God" (James 1:5).

Not every problem has a simple solution, and not every person has the same level of faith or understanding. Some problems are so rare and unique that the pastor cannot easily bring a godly word of counsel regarding them.

When my phone rang late one Saturday evening, I heard the anxious voice of a woman in my church. She asked if she and her husband could come immediately to our house to talk. "Of course, please come," I responded. "What's happened?"

"The police picked up my husband tonight," she explained. "We need to talk with you." My curiosity piqued, I put down the phone and waited. They arrived looking frightened, pale, and drawn.

After I prayed with them for God's help and wisdom, Rick, the young man, told me that he had been picked up and arrested for soliciting a prostitute. The story made my blood run cold. Why was a Christian man going alone downtown to an area that prostitutes frequent? Continuing, Rick said that he had gone downtown to share the gospel with the girls on the streets, citing his concern and compassion for women caught in the sex trade. He said that he had been picked up for talking to a prostitute but that he was innocent of any wrongdoing. Rick said that the police had made a false arrest and that he needed me to believe him and keep this confidential. His wife sat beside him, crying. She also pleaded with me to believe her husband. Then she added that she was pregnant with their first child.

After hearing their pleadings, I decided to believe Rick's story, but I wanted proof of his claims. I asked to see the police report as soon as it was available, and I promised to walk with them through the dark valley of this sad experience and keep it confidential. I prayed with them and sent them home. I went to bed but didn't sleep much.

In the next few days, I routinely checked back with Rick and his wife. Rick seemed to handle the upsetting circumstance without much anxiety. A court hearing before a judge was coming soon, and I wanted to see the police report before then, but Rick asked me to be patient, because the report was not ready. Days passed, and still no police report. I started to get uneasy because I knew from experience that police reports do not take weeks to file. Wisdom and experience were telling me that his story had flaws and that Rick was trying to keep me from seeing the truth.

Finally I said to Rick, "I need that report." Monday morning Rick dropped the police report on my desk in an envelope. He reassured me that he was innocent.

After Rick was gone I opened the envelope and read the report. I nearly fell out of my chair. Rick had been picked up talking to an undercover policewoman who had recorded their entire conversation! As I read the report, it became exceedingly clear that Rick had not been there to share Christ with a prostitute but to pay for her services. Rick had lied to me and to his wife and tried to cover up his wrongdoing by stalling.

The steps that I took in the next days required great wisdom. I needed to maintain the integrity of the church, find out if the arrest would be reported in the local news, help this couple save their marriage, and keep calm. What did I do? The first thing I did was cry out to God for wisdom. I was a young man myself, and I needed God's help and wisdom.

Without going into all the details, I can say that God answered my prayers for wisdom. The church kept its integrity, the story was not reported in the newspapers, Rick pled guilty and got probation, and, in time, his marriage was saved! All those outcomes required a generous load of God's wisdom.

Think It Over: Approach Problems Asking God for Wisdom

1. What counseling situations have you faced that were too hard for you to handle? Did you turn to God for His wisdom, or did

you handle the situation in your own wisdom? What were the results?

2. Commit to prayer and to searching out God's Word on difficult matters both when you are counseling people and when you are alone with the matter before God.

Approach Problems Hoping God Will Resolve Them

The sixth and final principle from this passage in James that we can apply to biblical counseling is to approach every problem with the hope that God will resolve it: "Let him ask God, who gives generously to all without reproach, and it will be given him" (James 1:5).

Every person with a problem, no matter how big or small, needs hope. The voices of despair get loud when problems are not easily or quickly resolved. "Will I ever get over this?" "Can I get my life back?" "Will I ever be forgiven?" "Can I trust my spouse again?" "Will I ever feel normal again?" The answer is a qualified yes. Hope does not return us to where we started. Hope takes us to a better place in God's plans for our future.

God says, "I know the plans I have for you, declares the Lord, plans for welfare and not for evil, to give you a future and a hope" (Jeremiah 29:11), and the psalmist reminds us, "His anger is but for a moment, and his favor is for a lifetime. Weeping may tarry for the night, but joy comes with the morning" (Psalm 30:5). One thing that every pastoral counselor can count on is that with God there is hope. Staying with God's Word, claiming God's promises, seeking God's wisdom is the path of hope.

I need to say a word to those who have been given extra grace from God to endure lifelong trials. God does not heal every disease or fix every problem this side of heaven. When God does not ordain to heal or bring resolution to a situation, we can count on one thing: where God allows ongoing suffering, God gives overcoming grace. For those who carry the pain of a child affected by a disability, a family member suffering with a mental illness, a loved one bearing an incurable condition, or any of a host of long-term "thorns in the flesh" (see 2 Cor. 12:7), I am confident that God's word is "My grace is sufficient for you, for my power is made perfect in weakness" (2 Corinthians 12:9). My wife and I have experienced this extra measure of God's grace taking care of our oldest daughter, who was born with a brain injury. This long and difficult path has been marked for us with emotional upsets and financial sinkholes, but God has always covered us with generous evidences of His miraculous grace.

The blessed hope is that one day all the pain, suffering, sickness, grief, and death will be things of the past. The former things will be forgotten, and God will make everything new. "He who was seated on the throne said, 'Behold, I am making all things new.' Also he said, 'Write this down, for these words are trustworthy and true'" (Revelation 21:5). To that I say a heartfelt "Amen!"

Think It Over: Approach Problems Hoping God Will Resolve Them

1. What are some of the long-term difficulties people have brought to you? What are some of the smaller matters?
2. In what ways can you offer hope to each person who comes to you with burdens, whether those burdens are big or small?

Some Practical Aspects of Pastoral Counseling

A pastor will face a myriad of issues over the course of his ministry. In my forty years as a pastor, I have dealt with a great many issues, including depression, anxiety, sexual abuse, sexual identity and homosexuality, infidelity and adultery, divorce and remarriage, domestic violence, addictions, fear, pre-marriage preparation, marital problems, child rearing and discipline, disputes over money, suicide, grief recovery, spiritual bondage, anger, broken trust, conflict resolution, and theft.

Not every pastor has the training, gifts, or temperament to make counseling a major part of his ministry, but every pastor is called to care for the flock. Because of this, one of the first things a pastor must determine is to what level he can offer counseling to the people in his congregation. Pastors with the spiritual gift of mercy or wisdom will excel in counseling, but those with leading or speaking gifts may not have a high level of success in functioning as a counselor. Every pastor is called to love and care for the flock, but not every pastor is equally equipped to administer healing and wise counsel.

Pastors with a high degree of natural gifting, wisdom, and compassion will discover that people will recognize those qualities and seek out the pastor for counsel. The pastor's temperament as seen in his teaching opens or closes the door for pastoral counseling. When a pastor shares openly and authentically about his struggles in his teaching and preaching, the flock perceives that their leader can identify with their pain and emotional battles. On the other hand, if a pastor never opens up his heart or shares his struggles with his church family, he will be perceived as closed and unsympathetic. Hurting people will tend to look for someone else to listen to them and give them counsel.

So what is required of the pastor when it comes to counseling? Below is a checklist that will help a pastor decide what level of counseling he should personally provide his congregation:

- Know yourself and your limitations.
- Gain a good grasp of biblical wisdom and insights.
- Listen carefully before drawing conclusions or offering solutions.
- Be non-judgmental with everyone but especially with people who are confused, who struggle, or who have failed miserably.
- Be tender and compassionate with those who are weak.
- Develop the ability to stay calm in all situations.
- Be careful to remain clear of emotional attachments.
- Understand your limitations, and don't go over the boundary.
- Be ready to refer long-term counseling to a professional.

Regardless of what level of counseling a pastor feels called to provide the individuals in his congregation, he can be helped in any counseling session by the use of good practices and resources:

- Pray before every counseling session, and pray with every counselee.
- Continually draw wisdom from the Bible—you will find it stated in principles and in the real stories of the Bible characters.
- Get acquainted with local resources that can assist your people: support groups, seminars, professional counselors, and hospitals.
- Get a copy of the *Christian Worker's Handbook* from the Billy Graham Evangelistic Association. It lists more than seventy Bible-based counseling guides on subjects ranging from abortion to pornography to suicide.

A final note of warning: despite the pastor's responsibility to care for his flock, counseling can bring with it challenges that can put a pastor in a vulnerable and even dangerous place. While it is essential that a pastor be available to his people at some level, it is also vital that he protect himself with certain safeguards:

- Be wise as to how much counseling you take on in order to avoid emotional fatigue.
- Maintain a strong and loving marriage.
- Keep yourself clear of emotional entanglements and maintain good ethical practices to protect your reputation. For example, a male pastor should not counsel a woman alone, a pastor should take someone with him when he goes to someone's house, and it is not wise for a pastor to go out late at night alone.
- Foster resources to help people in aftercare such as small support groups within the church.
- Know your limitations and when it's time to refer a person to someone better equipped than you are.

A pastor must carefully consider the wide range of needs that his people may face, his own gifting and limitations, and practices and resources that can help him in his counseling sessions; and he must consider the potential pitfalls inherent in counseling and safeguard himself against compromising situations. When a pastor wisely evaluates these issues and makes use of various helps, he will be well-equipped to care for his flock in the matter of counseling.

Think It Over: Some Practical Aspects of Pastoral Counseling

1. In what ways do you feel most prepared to do spiritual counseling? In what areas would you like more training to counsel?
2. In what types of counseling have you seen the greatest healing?
3. How do you use prayer in your counseling sessions?
4. For what common struggles do people most often request counseling from you?

5. What resources do you have to help you address people's most common problems? What resources do you wish you had to address these common problems? What do you need to do to get these resources?
6. What safeguards do you have in place to protect you from unwanted emotional dependencies with female counselees?

CONCLUSION:
The Pastoral Leader and Counseling

Whether a pastor is naturally gifted as a counselor or not, each pastor must learn biblical wisdom and use it as the foundation of all advice that he gives. He must learn to pray for himself and for the issues that others bring to him. He must learn his own limitations and stay within his abilities and gifting. It is far better to refer someone to a more experienced or trained counselor than to take on a messy situation and offer unwise counsel that only adds to the mess. The Hippocratic oath that doctors must take at medical school applies to pastors: "First do no harm."

9

The Pastoral Leader and Caring for the Flock

Objective: *To define the biblical relationship between a pastor and his people and to give practical principles on the role of shepherding.*

They don't care how much you know until they know how much you care." That guiding principle should be stamped on the heart of every spiritual leader. When the Holy Spirit inspired Paul to write out God's plan for the church, he put pastoring and teaching together as one gift: "He gave the apostles, the prophets, the evangelists, the shepherds and teachers" (Ephesians 4:11). The construction of that sentence in the Greek New Testament could just as easily read, "He gave the apostles, the prophets, the evangelists, the shepherds who are also teachers."

To separate the functions of teaching and shepherding the flock of God is unbiblical, because to separate them is unhealthy for the church. God's plan is not for pastors to put in a teaching performance on the weekend and then ignore the flock the rest of the week. Teaching and pastoral work are inseparably connected.

When I was a young pastor just out of school, a highly regarded veteran pastor said to me, "You can do more pastoring in five minutes than you can do in five years if you are there when the sheep need you." At first I wondered at such a statement, but now, after years of experience in local church ministry, I completely agree. Most believers in the local church are content to support and serve without much personal time or attention from the pastor. However, when they or their family members are faced with great celebration, such as a wedding or graduation, or with great tragedy, such as sickness or death, they need the pastor to be their shepherd. When a need arises, the people do not remember how great the pastor's last sermon was—they expect the pastor to be in personal contact with them.

When my son, Jon, was a little boy, we had an esteemed guest for dinner who was serving as the president of a nationally known seminary. I will never forget Jon's response as we welcomed the esteemed president known as "Doctor" to the front door and I introduced him to my son. Jon reached out his little hand to greet our guest and said, "Are you the kind of doctor who helps people or the kind who just reads books?" We all enjoyed a moment of nervous laughter, but my son's insight points to how some people perceive their pastor. If the flock perceives that the pastor loves books and study more than he loves people and personal interaction with them, the atmosphere of the church will suffer.

Carrying Out the Pastor's Tasks in Love

Studies in education have shown that the most important factor in motivating a student to learn is the relationship of the teacher to the student. While a pastor is required to carry out a number of biblical tasks, including preaching, the tasks of a shepherd will be easier to fulfill when the flock knows that the pastor cares about each of them personally.

What are the biblical tasks required of a pastor in caring for his flock?

- *Feed the flock.* "[Jesus] said to him, 'Feed my lambs'" (John 21:15). "Devote yourself to the public reading of Scripture, to exhortation, to teaching" (1 Timothy 4:13).
- *Preach the whole counsel of God from the Bible.* "I did not shrink from declaring to you the whole counsel of God" (Acts 20:27). "I became a minister according to the stewardship from God that was given to me for you, to make the word of God fully known" (Colossians 1:25).
- *Equip the people for ministry.* "[God] gave . . . shepherds and teachers, to equip the saints for the work of ministry, for building up the body of Christ" (Ephesians 4:11–12).

- *Work to make every believer mature in Christ.* "Him we proclaim, warning everyone and teaching everyone with all wisdom, that we may present everyone mature in Christ" (Colossians 1:28). "What you have heard from me . . . entrust to faithful men who will be able to teach others also" (2 Timothy 2:2).
- *Prepare and motivate believers to fulfill the Great Commission.* "Go therefore and make disciples of all nations" (Matthew 28:19).
- *Set a godly example for believers to follow.* "Set the believers an example in speech, in conduct, in love, in faith, in purity" (1 Timothy 4:12).
- *Pray for all the saints.* "Keep alert with all perseverance, making supplication for all the saints" (Ephesians 6:18). "Far be it from me that I should sin against the Lord by ceasing to pray for you" (1 Samuel 12:23).
- *Watch over the flock of God.* "Shepherd the flock of God that is among you, exercising oversight" (1 Peter 5:2). "[Jesus] said to him, 'Tend my sheep'" (John 21:16).

In the pursuit of these important goals, a pastor should never forget that achieving these goals is dependent on whether the flock feels that their shepherd cares for them. The flock should never doubt the love of their shepherd, and the shepherd should never relate to the flock without love. God's people do not desire a polished professional as much as they need a loving shepherd.

Pastoral concern is at the heart of pastoral success. It is easy for the pastor to fall into the trap of continually telling people what they should do and what they need to be and to forget to just love them for who they are!

The apostle Paul was likely the most determined missionary, articulate teacher, and busiest pastor who ever lived. For these reasons Paul is too often seen as a pushy, ambitious, and coldhearted preacher. However, take a closer look at his letters, and the pastor's heart of Paul is clear to see. Paul said to Timothy, "I remember you constantly in my prayers night and day. As I remember your tears, I long to see you, that I may be filled with joy" (2 Timothy 1:3–4). To Titus Paul wrote, "Greet those who love us in the faith. Grace be with you all" (Titus 3:15). To the church at Philippi, Paul exclaimed, "I hold you in my heart . . . for God is my witness, how I yearn for you all with the affection of Jesus Christ" (Philippians 1:7–8). Loving the flock means that a pastor constantly thinks about his people, prays for them, and enjoys being with them.

But not all members of the church are loveable or easy to lead. Sometimes people are difficult because no one has ever loved them. Breaking down the barriers that people erect in response to a history of hurt can become one of the pastor's finest achievements in ministry. At times, however, people leave a church and say terrible things about the church not being a loving place or the shepherd not being a loving man. A loveless reputation casts a cloud on anything good that a church may be known for.

In light of these difficulties, how does a pastor carry out his biblically appointed duties to his flock with the love and care needed to minister to people's needs? We'll spend the rest of the chapter looking at ways to do this.

Think It Over: Carrying Out the Pastor's Tasks in Love

1. Do you see yourself as mainly a teacher or as a pastor who teaches? What is the difference?
2. As the pastor/teacher, what do you do and say that reminds your followers that you love them?
3. How could you improve in what you say or do that would communicate your love for them?
4. Do you believe that your people love you? What feedback from the members of your flock shows that they know that you truly care about them?

Caring Pastors Know Their Sheep

Good pastors know their sheep. Knowing someone's name is only a start, but it's a good start. It's been said that calling someone by name is like giving that person a gift.

In my years as a youth pastor, I met a college-aged man who was a visitor at church. His name was not easy to remember or pronounce. Later that week as I was doing business at the city center, I saw him. I remembered his name and called out to him from a distance. He immediately turned around with a smile, and we had a brief but cordial conversation.

The next Sunday this man came back to church and said to me, "I was not planning to come back to your church, but when you remembered my name, I had to return." Decades later that man serves the Lord in that church, and he and I are still friends. Pastors who know the members of their flock by name are like Jesus who said, "My sheep hear my voice, and I know them, and they follow me" (John 10:27).

Think It Over: Caring Pastors Know Their Sheep

1. If someone in your church is facing a crisis, will they feel comfortable calling you? Will you feel comfortable receiving that call?
2. How well do you know the members of your congregation? What can you do to be more intentional about knowing people's names, families, and life situations?

Caring Pastors Pray for Their Sheep

A pastor is never closer to the sheep than when he carries them to the great Shepherd in prayer. But as was noted in the previous section, in order for a caring pastor to intercede for his flock, he needs to know the circumstances of the individuals in the flock. The ministry of intercession should come out of a sense of responsibility and love for the people. Praying for the people promotes a spiritual sensitivity to their needs and gives room for the Holy Spirit to prompt the pastor when a visit, a call, or a written note is needed.

A particular woman in my church was married to an unbeliever. When she came to worship, she had a strange habit of saving the seat next to her. When I asked her about it, she told me that she was saving the chair for her husband. She asked me to join her in prayer for her husband's salvation. So I started praying regularly for Roger.

Two years passed, and one day, as I sat in my office preparing a sermon, I felt the strongest urge to go to the local hospital. The inexplicable thing was that no one from my church was in the hospital, but the internal nudges would not stop, so I took it as the leading of the Holy Spirit. I traveled to the hospital thinking, *This is crazy—I don't know of anyone from my church who is in the hospital.*

When I arrived at the medical center, I walked through the door and met Roger's wife, who shouted to me, "How did you know?"

"Know what?" I replied, rather surprised.

"Roger was hit by a speeding car and is in the emergency room," she quickly explained. "The doctors do not expect him to live." My heart sank, because I knew that Roger was not a believer and that he was facing eternity without Christ. Quickly the woman led me into the room where her husband lay unconscious. Knowing that Roger's life was ebbing away, I prayed over him, asking God to spare his life and allow him to hear the gospel and be saved. God answers prayer. Roger lived and miraculously recovered from his nearly fatal injuries.

When he came out of the hospital, I went to see him. I told him how I had prayed for him for two years and that I had prayed over him at the hospital, asking God to spare his life. Then I asked him if he was ready to receive Christ by faith as his Savior and Lord. Roger enthusiastically said yes! I led him in the prayer to receive Christ, and the next Sunday and every Sunday following, Roger sat in church next to his wife in the seat that she had saved for him. God used my knowledge of this woman's personal circumstances to bring her husband to Christ.

Think It Over: Caring Pastors Pray for Their Sheep

1. How much do you know about the circumstances of the individuals in your church?
2. How regularly do you pray for people in your congregation by name? How can you increase your love and your prayer life for the various members of your church?

Caring Pastors Lovingly Correct Their Sheep

Sometimes God calls pastors to say hard things. A pastor's love makes rebuke and correction possible (see 2 Corinthians 2:4). St. Augustine said, "Love me, and then say anything to me about me."

When a pastor confronts a fellow believer, a few guiding principles apply:

- Prepare the setting by making an appointment in a neutral place. Typically the church building is a good place. If it involves a woman, make sure you have another godly woman present.
- Begin with prayer.
- Assure the person of the confidentiality of the meeting.
- Never start with an accusation. False accusations only inflame a situation.
- If you have conclusive evidence of wrongdoing, gently present the issue needing correction and then ask for a response. Bring correction from God's Word. Lead the person in a time of confession. Encourage him to walk worthy of his calling. Pray with and for his.
- If you do not have conclusive evidence of wrongdoing, ask, "Is it possible that I could have heard something about you that as your pastor would have distressed me?"
- If the person says, "I don't know what you're talking about," repeat the question and wait.
- If the person still does not answer, ask him, "Are you sure there isn't something?"
- Eventually the person will give some answer, but you may need to prompt him.
- When the issue is finally out, bring a word of correction from the Bible and then ask for a response. Lead the person in a time of confession. Encourage him. Pray with and for him.

When a pastor brings a word of correction, it is an act of love, even if it is not received well or is completely rejected. Sometimes a loving rebuke can provoke disgust and animosity, but that response indicates where the person's heart is.

Leland was twenty years old when both his parents died. He had no place to stay, so I invited him to live with my family until we could help him get out on his own. In the weeks that followed, I counseled Leland and helped him find a job and get a car. After a few months he was ready to move into his own apartment. His life was coming together.

A few months after this, I heard that Leland was having an affair with a married woman. After verifying the story I went to see Leland. When I confronted him about his sin, he became angry; he didn't want to discuss it, and our relationship went cold. It was heartbreaking to me, given the investment of time and mentoring that I had made in Leland.

I continued to pray for him. Months passed, and I heard that Leland had ended his immoral relationship with the married woman. One day I heard a knock at my door. When I opened it, I saw Leland standing there with a sad look on his face. I invited him in, and we sat down. Leland began to cry. He apologized for disappointing me and for getting involved in an immoral affair. Then Leland said something that I will never forget: "You loved me enough to tell me the truth. Thank you, pastor. I love you!"

Shepherds who care for their flock will love them enough to correct them (see 2 Timothy 4:2) and will be quick to praise them when praise is due (see 1 Corinthians 11:2). This is one way to keep the flock spiritually healthy.

Think It Over: Caring Pastors Lovingly Correct Their Sheep

1. Are you willing to bring a word of correction to your flock when it is biblically called for?
2. When you need to bring a word of correction to one of your flock, how will that person know that you love him?

Caring Pastors Visit Their Wounded Sheep

A caring pastor must enter into emotional circumstances in order to care for wounded sheep. Jesus made this clear in His teaching on the good shepherd: "What man of you, having a hundred sheep, if he has lost one of them, does not leave the ninety-nine in the open country, and go after the one that is lost, until he finds it? And when he has found it, he lays it on his shoulders, rejoicing" (Luke 15:4–5). Life is unpredictable, so caring pastors need to understand that people get sick, find themselves in tragic situations, and face the valley of the shadow of death. When unexpected trouble comes to the sheep, they need the shepherd's care.

When a pastor visits people in the hospital, at home, or in a nursing home, it will be a blessing to them if the pastor follows these simple rules:

- Make your visits brief. Long visits wear patients out. Sick people feel as if they have to use all their energy for the pastor.
- Touch them. Unless the person has a communicable infection, touch him on the hand or arm. Often people in hospitals feel isolated and alone because of the lack of human touch.
- Bring a short word of encouragement from God's Word. Have some of God's promises memorized so that you can quote them.
- Before you pray for the person, ask, "How would you like me to pray for you?"
- Smile and look at the person before you leave. Your face and eyes communicate care when words fail.
- If you go to a hospital room and the patient is not there, leave your business card or a note to tell the person that you were there. Write that you were praying for him.
- If the person you were visiting is unconscious, make sure that you have a one-way conversation with him. Speak directly to the person in a soft voice near his ear. Remind him of God's presence with him and pray for him. Never talk about the person as if he were not there.

When visiting someone whom you know is near death, be prepared to speak with him about heaven. Here are some simple rules to follow:

- Don't be afraid to talk candidly about dying. Most people who are dying understand that their grip on this life is fading. They need reassurance from God's Word.
- Remind the person of the gospel and of the hope of everlasting life based on faith in Christ alone and not on works. One of Satan's last attacks is to cause a believer to fear that he has not done enough to enter heaven.
- Explain to the person what the Bible says about the process of dying: "Absent from the body and present with the Lord" (2 Corinthians 5:8). Tell the person that his last conscious memory on Earth will be his first conscious memory in heaven.
- Read a comforting passage from the Bible to him such as John 14:1–4.

- Listen for any last words.
- Touch the person and pray over him, committing him to the Lord.
- Leave quietly.

As a church grows larger, pastoral care and visitation must be organized, systematic, and shared among all the church leadership. When the need for visitation and pastoral care grows beyond the leadership of the church, a specialized ministry of visitation and care needs to be launched. At Cornerstone Church we have specially trained visitation volunteers who go out with the blessing of the church leadership.

A caring pastor can learn something profound from a medical doctor. A skilled physician carefully observes and listens to his patient before making a diagnosis. Then with insight and experience he administers life-giving care. A caring pastor will discern the wounded sheep's need through careful observation and listening. Then with a loving touch, spiritual wisdom from God's Word, and powerful praying, the pastor can fulfill the task of being an under-shepherd of Jesus, the great Shepherd of the sheep.

Think It Over: Caring Pastors Visit Their Wounded Sheep

1. When you visit the sick, what Bible promises will you have memorized that will minister to them?
2. What is your plan to organize and train others to visit the sick and aged?
3. Who will manage the visitation ministry at your church so that everyone who needs a call will get one?

Caring Pastors Celebrate with Their Sheep

The work of shepherding the flock of God is grueling and exhausting, but it also brings times of joy, rejoicing, and celebration. The caring pastor is called to weep with those who weep, but he is also called to rejoice with those who rejoice. When someone in the flock experiences a reason to celebrate, the pastor can be there to add his voice of praise to God for a special blessing.

Many events lend themselves to a pastoral presence at a celebration. Some of the festivities and commemorations at which a pastor can rejoice with those who rejoice are these:

- The birth of a child
- Engagement to be married
- Marriage
- Baptism
- School graduation
- Sporting events
- Musical recitals
- A work promotion
- The dedication of a new house
- Retirement
- Opening a new business
- Special wedding anniversaries
- Special birthdays
- An award for community service
- The election of a politician
- An award in education
- Achievement in business

At many of these events, the pastor's presence is sufficient as a statement of his love and support. Other events call for the pastor to be directly involved in officiating or participating in a celebration. Either way, rejoicing with the flock connects the pastor to the sheep in a healthy and happy way. Building happy memories together helps carry both the pastor and the people through hard times. Too often a pastor is only present in times of trouble or tragedy; when that is the case, people's perception of the pastor's role is imbalanced. Attending the celebration of a member of the church may not seem highly important to a pastor, but it is a big honor to his people, and it binds them to their shepherd.

The caring pastor has a big advantage over the preacher who chooses not to get involved in the lives of his flock. While Christians respect a preacher who declares the truth and fulfills his duties in the pulpit, they will not necessarily love him or feel a personal connection to him as their leader. The caring pastor has the respect *and* love of his flock, because the flock knows that their pastor truly loves them.

Think It Over: Caring Pastors Celebrate with Their Sheep

1. What joyful events have you attended or officiated at in the past month?
2. Why do you think that rejoicing with those who rejoice is important to being a caring pastor?

CONCLUSION:
The Pastoral Leader and Caring for the Flock

Jesus said, "I am the good shepherd. I know my own and my own know me, just as the Father knows me and I know the Father; and I lay down my life for the sheep" (John 10:14–15). Jesus shepherds His flock with personal knowledge of His sheep, and His sheep follow Him with personal knowledge of their good Shepherd. Jesus is the ultimate model for pastors who desire to lead their flock well.

10

The Pastoral Leader and Church Organization

Objective: *To provide a clear and simple-to-understand organizational structure for a church using the six elements of organizational architecture and give insights on how to keep a church or organization young and missions focused.*

Pastors are expected to lead, but often pastors do not know how to put the various pieces of the ministry together. Many are thrust into their leadership position without any idea of how to organize a church. Oftentimes a pastor feels like an engineering student in his first year of school who is required to plan and build a skyscraper, or like a small child who has had a complicated Lego set dumped on the floor in front of him.

Some pastors inherit an organization that was already in place when they arrived as the leader. They just do their best to keep it going. They may instinctively know that the organization is not working, but they are too fearful of rocking the boat to do anything about it. Often pastors leading a new or dysfunctional church feel frustrated by the disorganization and lack of structure or direction.

For many years of my pastoral ministry, I read books on vision, strategy, goal setting, and organizing a church. It seemed as if every book had a different angle on these topics, and the authors' definitions of key terms were inconsistent and sometimes incomprehensible. Some books overemphasized the organic nature of the church as the body of Christ and stressed a "just let it happen" approach. Others overemphasized corporate theory, and I felt as if I were reading material by Wall Street consultants. After years of being a pastor, I felt like that first-year engineering student or the toddler with a Lego set. What I needed was a simple explanation of how a church or Christian ministry should be organized and some understandable definitions.

With a sincere desire to make this topic simple and clear, I will attempt in this chapter to give some definition to church organizational theory.

I have found that the key to organizational leadership is the alignment of six elements that form an organization's architecture: mission, vision, values, strategic direction, strategic plans, and structure. These six elements can be compared to the organization of the human body:

- *Mission* is the person's purpose for living.
- *Vision* represents the eyes and imagination of the body seeing a bright place to go in the future.
- *Values* are the clothes that cover and protect the body.
- *Strategic direction* means mapping out the road ahead.
- *Strategic plans* are the body's individual steps forward on the road ahead.
- *Structure* is the body's skeleton, which keeps everything in place while walking or running.

Let's take a closer look at these key ingredients of church organization.

The Church's Mission

Mission is the fundamental reason why the church or Christian organization exists and is a statement of what it wants to ultimately accomplish. It is the basic statement of purpose. The church's mission should be clear, compelling, and concise so that everyone in the church can state it, feel it in their hearts, and want to accomplish it.

In 2001 I prayerfully sat at a table with a blank piece of paper in front of me. After years of effective ministry in two countries, God had called me to plant a new church. I could easily have drawn on the past, since I was experienced in writing mission statements. I knew that most mission statements had the same three elements expressed in different language. For example, one I had seen read, "Win them, build them, and send them," while another had declared, "Reach up, reach in, and reach out."

But as I sat staring at the blank paper, I knew that this time was different. I asked the Lord what His mission was for our church, and in answer to my prayers, the Lord surprised me with a mission statement that I hadn't expected—the acrostic L.E.A.D. It stood for love God, equip believers, answer God's call, and declare the good news.

The Lord showed me that, first and foremost, the mission of a church is not to make disciples but to love God and love people. At Cornerstone Church our primary mission from the beginning has been not about growing a great organization but rather helping people to know and love the God who already loves them perfectly. In Matthew 22:37–39 Jesus answered the question of why we exist by telling us the greatest commandments: "Love the Lord your God with all your heart and with all your soul and with all your mind. This is the first and greatest commandment. And a second is like it: You shall love your neighbor as yourself." Starting from the foundation of love made everything else in Cornerstone's mission make sense.

The second part of our mission addressed the need for every believer to grow in Christ. At Cornerstone equipping every believer is absolutely essential, because the church's survival depends on it. What is the goal of equipping? Ephesians 4:13 gives us the answer: "the whole measure of the fullness of Christ" (NIV). Simply put, an equipped Christian thinks and lives like Jesus.

The third element of our mission was for people to answer God's call to serve. Jesus said, "The greatest among you shall be your servant" (Matthew 23:11). Over the next few years we learned to answer the important question, what will it take to answer God's call to serve? We learned the four golden rules for servants who answer God's call:

1. Look around you for an opportunity to serve (see John 9:1–4).
2. Serve in a ministry tailored for you (see Ephesians 2:10).
3. Approach your service with humility (see John 13:13–17).
4. Let love for God motivate your service (see Revelation 2:2–5).

Finally, Cornerstone's mission called God's people to declare the good news of the gospel to the world. The essence of the Christian message is the good news of God's love and forgiveness offered by grace alone through faith alone in God's only Son, Jesus Christ. Romans 10:9 gives this guarantee: "If you confess with your mouth that Jesus is Lord and believe in your heart that God raised him from the dead, you will be saved." Cornerstone Church believes the gospel, communicates the gospel, lives the gospel, and is not ashamed of the gospel, because it is the power of God to transform everyone who believes it (see Romans 1:16).

With the four points taken together to create the word L.E.A.D., our mission statement is easy to remember: love God, equip believers, answer God's call, and declare the good news. Mission statements need to be biblically sound, inspiring, brief, and easy for the entire church to remember.

Several questions help define mission:

- Why do we exist?
- What is our main purpose?
- What specific task(s) has God given us to do?
- What rationale can we give for our church or organization's life?

Think It Over: The Church's Mission

1. How would you describe your church or organization if it were a physical body?
   a. Standing straight and tall
   b. Stumbling backward without muscle coordination
   c. Leaning and about to fall
   d. Loose at the joints
   e. Moving but breathing hard
   f. Other______________________
2. In a few words, what is the mission of your church or organization?
3. If your church or organization did not exist, what great purpose would not get done?
4. Is your mission clear, or does it need work?
5. What percentage of your church knows the church's mission?

The Church's Vision

Vision is the leadership's view of where the church or Christian organization is going in the future. It is built around the most desirable future for the organization. It is always guided by and aligned with the mission.

Vision involves imagining the future and projecting the organization's overall direction into that desired future. The mission never changes, but the vision can change as the church advances in its mission.

An exciting vision of a church's future provides the necessary fuel to take the church to its next milestone. Vision statements are aspirations of what a brighter future will look like. A growing church will need to keep its vision current by regularly evaluating what it has accomplished and what overall goals it should attempt to achieve.

When Cornerstone Church began, neither I nor anyone on our leadership team could see the bright future and world impact that God had planned for us. Some of the technologies that we now use each week to reach over thirty countries with a Livestream broadcast had not yet been invented! Vision needs to keep pace with the newest opportunities that God presents.

These questions help define vision:

- If we could choose our best future, what would it look like?
- What is the brightest future for our church or Christian organization that we can imagine?
- Where do we want to be in one year, five years, or ten years?

Think It Over: The Church's Vision

1. What do you see as the vision? What brighter future is motivating you and the church?
2. What is the brightest future for your church or Christian organization that you can imagine?
3. Where do you want to be in one year, five years, or ten years?

The Church's Values

Values refer to the norms, ideals, and ethical standards that guide the behavior of the church or Christian organization. Values are designed to guide and protect people as they work together. Values remind everyone that the church organization is more than boxes on an organizational chart. Values influence the policy decisions that leaders make and the way everyone interacts with each other.

When Cornerstone began, we chose five values to guide the behavior of our church: authentic community, active prayer, biblical focus, empowered believers, and effective outreach. These church values show up in three areas: first, in what we consider to be top priority; second, in how people relate to one another; and third, in how the church spends both human and financial resources. Church values help leaders make decisions about what goals to set, what priorities to keep, and what things will need financial and human resources.

The following questions help define values:

- What are the main ideals and standards that guide us?
- What moral principles most influence how we work together?
- What biblical beliefs give us boundaries that protect us from behaving in a way that will damage the church or Christian organization?

Think It Over: The Church's Values

1. What are the main ideals and standards that guide your church or organization?
2. What moral principles most influence how you and the members of your church work together?
3. What biblical beliefs give you boundaries that protect you from behaving in a way that will damage the church or Christian organization?

The Church's Strategic Direction

Strategic direction is the map of the future. It lays out the church's plan to accomplish the mission and vision, and it takes into account the environment surrounding the overall plan for growth.

Here is how it fits together: Think of yourself as an archer ready to release an arrow. Mission provides you the target, vision tells you where to aim, and strategic direction is the path that the arrow will take. The strategic direction tells the church or organization, "Given our assumptions about the needs, available resources, and changes in our environment, this is the direction we need to take in order to accomplish our mission and move toward our future vision."

In 2001 Cornerstone Church began by meeting in a rented school auditorium. It was not long, however, before we realized that the school in which we met was in crisis. The district administration was considering closing the facility, where most of the children came from the poorest neighborhoods in Long Beach. Failing test scores and campus violence threatened to close this school that had been operating for more than fifty years.

Though Cornerstone was in its first weeks as a church, God led us to pray and help this public school by tutoring the children, giving food to hungry families, offering new school uniforms, purchasing school supplies, and much more. The new principal and his staff were so encouraged by the involvement of people from our church that campus morale changed. Within five years this school that had been in crisis was given the United States' highest award for academic achievement!

This miraculous turnaround was truly a work of God through a church committed to a strategic direction. Today Cornerstone Church has an open door to our local public schools, and we have ministries in ten of them.

Several questions help define strategic direction:

- Where do we go next?
- Given our mission, vision, values, and resources, what overall direction should we set for our church?
- What is our next big destination on the road we are on?

Think It Over: The Church's Strategic Direction

1. What major direction is next for your church?
2. Given your mission, vision, values, and resources, what overall direction should be set for your church?
3. What is the next strategic destination on the road you are on?

The Church's Strategic Plans

Strategic plans are the specific goals a church or organization wants to accomplish in a given period of time. Effective strategic plans have clear indicators embedded in the goals. They tell the organization the steps and stages that it will take to accomplish its mission and vision.

Strategic plans identify and align the resources that will be used, both human and financial. Plans give specific times as to when progress will to be done and how achievement will be measured. They are shorter term than strategic direction. Strategic direction provides the map, while strategic objectives pinpoint the milestones.

Six principles should guide a pastor when setting goals and strategic plans. Strategic plans should be:

- Significant enough to be worthwhile
- Simple enough to be understood and fulfilled
- Short enough to be memorable
- Sensible enough to be achievable
- Specific enough to be measurable
- Spiritual enough to be eternal

The well-worn management principle states, "If you aim at nothing, you will be sure to hit it." Growing churches need to give time and thought to the practical steps that will get them to their next level. Setting goals that align with the church mission and that are memorable and measureable will allow leaders to evaluate progress, make adjustments, and form plans for the future. At Cornerstone I require every staff member to submit a statement of their ministry goals for each year. This practice has made it much easier for us to manage and forecast the next steps for Cornerstone's future.

Several questions help define strategic plans:

- How will we get to our next destination?
- What steps do we need to take to get there?
- How can we measure our progress?
- What resources will we need to get us to the next milestone?

Think It Over: The Church's Strategic Plans

1. What is your plan to get your church to the next major growth level?
2. What measureable steps do you need to take to get there?

3. How will you measure progress?
4. What resources will be needed to get your church to the next milestone?

The Church's Structure

Structure refers to how the church or Christian organization is controlled and coordinated. Structure answers questions about who reports to whom, what policy boundaries apply, what role each person plays, and where responsibility lies. When questions need to be answered about how the organization works, the structure should have the answer.

Churches are governed and organized in a variety of ways, but what every church must have in its structure is clarity. The best structure is one in which lines of authority, avenues of communication, and boundaries set by policies are well understood by everyone in advance. The organizational structure is of special importance when disagreements arise over who is in charge, who is responsible, and who is accountable.

These questions help define structure:

- What roles and responsibilities does each leader have and not have?
- What is our accountability scheme? Who answers to whom?
- What are the boundaries that keep everyone in line and everything running smoothly?
- What is our organizational chart, and how is to be interpreted?

One of the most important tools in building a strong and enduring organizational structure is delegation. The acrostic D.I.D.—duplicate, inspire, and delegate—will help every pastoral leader understand the path to effective delegation.

Good leaders know that in order to successfully move a church organization forward they must identify people in whom they can *duplicate* themselves and their work. People who have the gifts and inclination to be mentored are invaluable to the forward progress of the growing church, because they multiply the impact of a church. Leaders must then *inspire* those in whom they will invest themselves before they can expect to *delegate* the work.

Below are some things to remember when delegating:

- Clearly articulate to people your desired outcome. Begin your explanation with the end in mind, and specify your desired results.
- Clearly identify any constraints or boundaries to the project. Where are the lines of authority, responsibility, and accountability? Should the person you are delegating wait to be told what to do? Ask what to do? Recommend what should be done and then act? Act and then report results to you immediately? Initiate action and then report to you periodically?
- Include people in the delegation process. Empower them by asking their input on what tasks should be delegated to them and when.
- Match the amount of responsibility you give a person with the amount of authority you give that individual. Understand that you can delegate your responsibility while still maintaining accountability for the end result.
- Delegate at the grassroots level of the organizational structure. The people who are closest to the work are the ones best suited for the task, because they have the most intimate knowledge of the everyday requirements for the task.
- Ensure the ministry's success through ongoing communication with and monitoring of the people you delegate.
- Focus on results. Allow the people you delegate some freedom on methods and processes.
- Delegate with established timelines and deadlines. Agree on a schedule of checkpoints for when progress will be reviewed. Make adjustments as necessary.

The road to a healthy church body that is organized and ready to accomplish its mission is sometimes long and rough. Pastors who are exceptional leaders will train every church leader on the basic definitions of organization and will persevere in applying them consistently. Just as the human body is a living organism that is organized, so the church, the body of Christ, must be organized to live, grow, and fulfill its divine purpose.

Think It Over: The Church's Structure

1. What roles and responsibilities does each leader in your church have and not have?
2. What is your church's accountability scheme? Who answers to whom?
3. What are the boundaries that keep everyone in line and everything running smoothly?
4. Describe or create your organizational chart and how it should be interpreted.
5. Who are the people you have marked out to duplicate yourself, inspire, and delegate?
6. What fears do you have in making organizational changes?
7. What greater effectiveness could be achieved if positive change comes?

How Movements Are Different from Institutions

While organization is important, it is vital to remember that the church is more than simply an organization. It is a movement of God. And one of the dangers of any movement of God is the tendency to think that organization is the key to success. Organization should serve to advance the church, of course, but the church should not serve the organization. When churches lose their passion for their mission and begin to rest on their organizational structure, they inevitably move toward their demise.

To retain a church's original passion and life, a pastor needs to understand the lifecycle of an organization. That is, while organizations generally begin with vision and enthusiasm, with the passage of time, most lose their original passion for their mission. Even as the signs of success are all around them, at some point they start down the long slide toward institutional death. To avoid the likelihood of his church becoming another dying institution, the exceptional pastoral leader must guard against losing the essence of what made the church great.

What factors keep a church progressing as an exciting movement and not dying slowly as an institution? One approach to answering that question is to learn from the wider study of social movements. It is important to discover what factors effective social movements have in common and what factors differentiate them from dying institutional organizations.

The following ten insights I gleaned from a national church growth conference in 2012. They are adapted from the research of Dr. George Hunter III, the distinguished professor emeritus of Asbury Theological Seminary's School of World Mission and Evangelism.[1] These insights, which Dr. Hunter has also explained in his book *The Recovery of a Contagious Methodist Movement*, have powerful implications for the leadership of churches or Christian organizations:

1. A movement is an organized network of people who share essentially the same definition of reality, the same message, and the same cause and objectives. Movements that feature a scattered message or pluralism never seem to have enough glue to stay together over the long haul.
2. A movement is not confined to a single campaign. The people are committed for as long as it takes.
3. A movement is distinct from a mere trend, because movements are minimally organized. Compared to institutions, however, movements are organized more from the bottom up than from the top down, they are more decentralized than centralized, and the movement's local organizations are more autonomous.
4. Within effective movements multiple organized micro-movements usually flourish. Serious movements encourage the proliferation of new micro-movements within the movement.
5. Movements usually lack the leverage of power typically present in an institutional organization. They rely on human relations, persuasion, and staying on message until the wider organization or society finally gets it.
6. Effective movements persuade everyone about their mission and the cause that drives the movement. The single-most important factor in whether the movement's mission will ultimately prevail depends on increasing the ranks of seriously committed members. Nominal members and free riders are liabilities. If the movement is perceived as small or declining, or its members are not perceived as serious, the movement is not taken seriously.

7. Effective movements continually look for ways to widen their scope and influence and to increase their range of programs and activities while abandoning programs and activities that are no longer effective.
8. In strong movements many members root their self-identity, at least partly, in their identification with the movement.
9. Effective movements are fairly flexible. They can change as they learn, as they grow, and as the context changes.
10. Effective movements communicate their vision and message in two steps: First, they communicate their message publicly, in as many ways as possible. Second, the movement's members then engage people who know about the movement in conversation and invitation.

The following diagram illustrates this lifecycle of a movement that eventually becomes an institution:

Think It Over: How Movements Are Different from Institutions

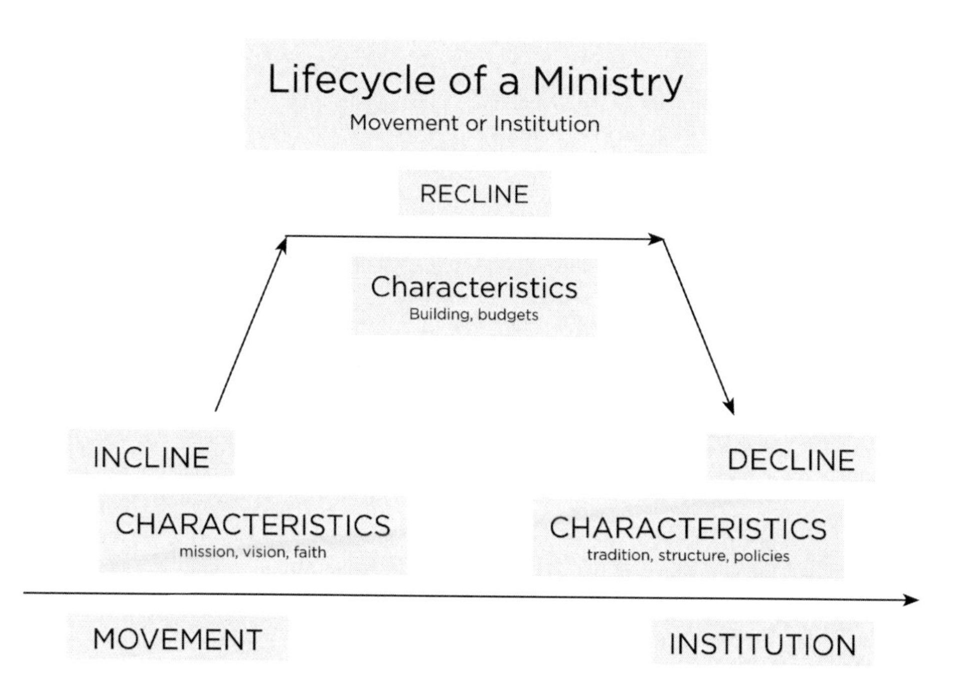

1. Rate your church or organization in terms of how much it is like a movement and how much it is like an institution.
2. What will you do to keep the movement fresh?

CONCLUSION:
The Pastoral Leader and Church Organization

Regardless of how much business acumen a pastor may have, a well-thought out organizational structure is important for any church. When the six elements that form an organization's architecture—mission, vision, values, strategic direction, strategic plans, and structure—are in place, it will clarify a church's goals and ministries. At the same time, a pastor must be careful never to allow organization to take over the original vision of the church. It is only as God's Spirit works in and through a church that its vision can be kept alive and it can work effectively in the lives of people.

11

The Costs and Blessings of Being a Pastoral Leader

Objective: *To warn and also encourage the pastor and his family regarding the high costs and unique benefits they will experience in spiritual leadership.*

The life of a pastoral leader is a mix of highs and lows reminiscent of the opening lines from Charles Dickens's novel *A Tale of Two Cities*: "It was the best of times, it was the worst of times." As we come to the final chapter of this study on pastoral leadership, it is vital to remember that while the cost of leadership is high, there is no doubt that its blessings ultimately outweigh its expense and sacrifice. As Jesus promised, "Everyone who has left houses or brothers or sisters or father or mother or children or lands, for my name's sake, will receive a hundredfold and will inherit eternal life" (Matthew 19:29).

The history of the church cannot be told without stories of heroism, faith, boldness, and daring. Untold numbers of leaders have sacrificed things that they considered most dear for the sake of following Christ. For some the cost was paid in their own blood. As I write this, I am at the Tyndale House in Cambridge, England, named after William Tyndale, whose courageous act of translating the New Testament into English was deemed such heresy that he was strangled and then burned at the stake. While martyrdom may not be the norm for pastors or leaders, personal sacrifice is required of every pastor.

On the other hand, there is no greater joy or reward than that found in the service of the Lord. After long prayer and seeking of the Lord, pastoral leaders have seen sweeping moves of God's power in which many came to repentance and faith in Christ. We see examples of this in the 1727 Moravian revival in what is now Germany, in Wales in 1905, and in the Scottish Hebrides in 1949. Pastors and leaders throughout biblical history have also experienced the joys of having deep ties with each other, receiving generously from God's people, and seeing miracles unfold before them, among other gifts.

Let's look at some of the expected sacrifices and blessings of leadership.

The Cost of Loneliness

Leadership requires that the leader be out in front of his followers. At times that is a lonely place. A scan of the Bible's great leaders reveals how they were forced into times of isolation as part of God's plan. Noah was alone in preaching of coming judgment, Abraham was called to leave his father's household, Joseph was betrayed by his brothers and left alone in a pit, Moses climbed Mount Sinai all alone to be with God, Daniel served God as an exile in foreign lands, Paul went away to Arabia as preparation for his ministry, and John was exiled to the island of Patmos. Not every pastor's life will be as dramatic as these men's lives were, but loneliness is a price that a pastor will pay in spiritual leadership.

Sometimes leaders must make crucial decisions that impact the lives of many of their followers. Those decisions are not always welcome, and a pastor must sacrifice the approval of those who follow him. Pastors who dare to preach prophetically will find themselves in a lonely place. Speaking a prophetic message cuts across the spirit of the times and requires that the preacher stand alone and unafraid. Leaders can readily welcome the support and friendship of colleagues and supporters, but a pastor must not need public affirmation so badly that it compromises his courage to take a stand when God's Word or God's leading is on the line.

Think It Over: The Cost of Loneliness

1. When do you feel most lonely in leadership?
2. Who are your closest and most loyal friends?
3. How does God use our times alone to make us better leaders?

The Cost of Misunderstandings, Hurt, and Betrayal

It is a leader's wake-up call to read the life of Paul. No man was more completely devoted to reaching the world for Christ than Paul was, yet he suffered the emotional pain of being misunderstood, hurt, and betrayed. Paul planted churches throughout the Roman world on three missionary journeys that required him to travel over ten thousand miles under stressful conditions. After a life of sacrifice evangelizing cities and appointing elders, in his farewell letter written from prison, Paul said, "You are aware that all who are in Asia turned away from me" (2 Timothy 1:15).

As a leader, I know the pain of being misunderstood, misquoted, and misrepresented. The most difficult of all personal hurt is betrayal. Leaders must trust those who work closely with them, but trust always leaves room for betrayal. Speaking from personal experience, betrayal ranks very high on the cost of leadership. Jesus experienced the searing pain of betrayal as a prelude to His crucifixion. Judas quickly comes to mind, but don't forget that all the disciples ran from Jesus at His arrest. John Mark was in such a panic to disassociate himself from Jesus that he apparently ran away naked! Later Peter denied Jesus three times, and Jesus felt the pain of his actions.

Betrayal may come to the most devoted pastor, but he must beware self-pity. A pastor must avoid this attitude like the plague—it is a sign of weakness and of a leader's potential misunderstanding of the nature of ministry. The ministry is not about the pastor but about Jesus. Hurt happens, but healing and reconciliation are God's sweet reversal. Endure hurt, and expect healing.

Think It Over: The Cost of Misunderstandings, Hurt, and Betrayal

1. In what ways have you been hurt or betrayed?
2. When Jesus was arrested His disciples fled; Paul was deserted by some Christians when he was imprisoned. What can you learn from their examples?
3. Why is self-pity so dangerous to a leader?

The Cost of Overexposure

Leaders stand out from the crowd, and therefore the crowd, made up of both followers and detractors, can easily observe what a leader says or does.

Public exposure is sometimes the result of curious and well-meaning people who just want to get a closer look inside the pastor's life and family. As a young pastor, I lived for a time in a house without a backyard fence. One evening a man from the church walked up to the back of the house, cupped his hands around his eyes, and peered through my windows. The shock of seeing an invited man looking into our house frightened my children. The unexpected visit was harmless and sparked by curiosity, but it felt like an intrusion to my family. Sometimes a leader's family pays the price of public exposure.

With their life and message, leaders put themselves into the arena of debate and disagreement. E-mails, letters, and angry phone calls of disagreement create rogue waves and powerful undercurrents that swirl around a leader, making his life uncomfortable. A good leader should never shrink from answering these communications while speaking the truth in love. To declare God's Word on unpopular moral stands is part of being exposed. If the pastor's pulpit is silent on current moral and spiritual issues, people will assume that the leader is either ignorant, intimidated, or in agreement with the status quo. The price of being public includes taking a stand and living with the consequences.

Public failure is a leader's most uncomfortable means of exposure. Pastors have faults that push their way into the open for all to see. Pastors are not infallible in their speech, their decisions, or their personal lives. Errors in judgment, exaggeration in speech, or failure to perform can create an environment of mistrust. The problem is not whether a pastor's fault will be known; it is more about what the pastor does when he fails. Every great leader must be prepared to quickly and humbly admit a fault or failure. The damage is done when leaders attempt to cover up failure or make excuses for their faults.

Think It Over: The Cost of Overexposure

1. What makes you feel most uncomfortable about being exposed to the public?
2. What can you do to protect your family?
3. How will you handle adverse publicity?

The Cost of Criticism

Even the most virtuous leader has critics and detractors who look for an opportunity to entrap him. The religious authorities criticized Jesus and looked for a way to snag Him. If critics harassed Jesus, the sinless Son of God, the pastor can be sure that critics will point an accusing finger at him also (see Luke 11:53–54; John 8:6).

Not every leader will have persistent open critics, but every leader will have two types of critics. First, there are people who love to criticize. These critics have a personal hatred of the leader because they despise his message or what he represents. Jesus directly confronted this kind of critic, and the leader must do the same, while keeping himself clear of entrapment. Second, there are people who are loving critics. Sometimes a perfectionistic but loyal follower will point out the mistakes in the leader. A wise leader will see this as an opportunity to make a friend and let the moment become an "iron sharpens iron" learning experience (see Proverbs 27:17).

In every case of criticism, the wise leader will take into account where the criticism is coming from, attempt to understand what is motivating it, and take an inventory of himself to see if he can use the criticism to improve. Sometimes a pastor will choose to wisely ignore tiny criticisms. Great leaders rise above criticism and use critics to make them better. Some great leaders who are criticized are not appreciated until they are gone. Then people build monuments to them with the stones they threw at them.

Think It Over: The Cost of Criticism

1. What can you learn from your critics?
2. How will you handle someone who falsely accuses you?
3. What does "iron sharpens iron" mean?

The Cost of Family Difficulties

The price that a pastor's family pays often goes unnoticed and unappreciated by followers. It is impossible to describe the myriad ways that the spouse and children of a pastor are affected. Here are some examples:

- Family members are expected to answer difficult questions asked by followers that are meant for the pastor.
- Spouses are required to be present and involved in ministry.
- Children must give up time with parents for the sake of the ministry.
- Family schedules must flex to make room for church emergencies.
- Children are disliked because of their parent's role in the community.
- Growing up in the spotlight is hard for the children of a pastor.
- A pastor is emotionally and physically fatigued, leaving little energy for his family.

The people closest to the pastor inevitably pay costly installments of sacrifice, but the families of great leaders pay the greatest price. However, if the pastor is godly and wise, his family will have a ringside seat to seeing how great leaders accomplish much and confront even the most difficult tasks and people. In that way the leader's family is an incubator for future leaders.

Think It Over: The Cost of Family Difficulties

1. How do your spouse and your children feel about their place in your life and in your leadership role?
2. What price has your family paid for you to be a pastor?
3. How have you thanked your family for their sacrifices?

The Cost of Time and Energy

One of the disadvantages that great pastors experience is never being able to mentally leave work. The emotional expense takes a toll on the physical energy of the leader.

The relationship between physical fatigue and mental exhaustion can be seen in Paul's description of his ministry experience: "In toil and hardship, through many a sleepless night, in hunger and thirst, often without food, in cold and exposure. And, apart from other things, there is the daily pressure on me of my anxiety for all the churches" (2 Corinthians 11:27–28). The level of responsibility and the need to anticipate the next step can drain a leader's time and energy both on and off the job.

Jesus, the greatest leader of all time, experienced excruciating physical fatigue and emotional exhaustion. When Jesus encountered the Samaritan woman, He was physically exhausted: "Jesus, wearied as he was from his journey, was sitting beside the well" (John 4:6). When Jesus was at the height of His popularity, He healed the sick and fed the five thousand, and the euphoric crowd wanted to make Him king. But Jesus, by now emotionally exhausted, withdrew to the mountain to pray (see John 6:15). The loss of time and emotional energy is a cost of leadership, so taking time away to refresh and renew is essential.

Think It Over: The Cost of Time and Energy

1. What kinds of things emotionally drain you?
2. When you are emotionally fatigued, what most recharges you?
3. What can you do to lift some of the stress off your life?
4. What do you need to add or subtract to balance your schedule?

The Cost of Spiritual Warfare and Internal Battles

A price that cannot be overlooked in the life of a pastor is the cost of fully engaging in the spiritual battle that surrounds a Christian leader. Satan knows that he can inflict heavy damage on the church if he can discourage, debase, or deceive a Christian leader. That is why the Christian leader is always under siege with one of Satan's three main schemes: deception, temptation, or accusation.

The first battle strategy of Satan is *deception*. He attacks pastors with well-orchestrated lies and deceits designed to defeat and discourage. The devil uses slander and divisiveness. This is why Jesus called Satan "the father of lies" (John 8:44). Satan's favorite lies tempt pastors to believe something false about God—to doubt God's plan, wisdom, or love. He lies about who God is and what God is doing or not doing. A leader always needs to be on guard with "the sword of the Spirit, which is the word of God" (Ephesians 6:17).

The second strategy of Satan is *temptation*. Typically Satan's temptations fall into the three basic categories described in 1 John 2:16: "All that is in the world—the desires of the flesh and the desires of the eyes and pride of life—is not from the Father but is from the world." These three classifications of temptation are pleasure, possessions, and pride. Another familiar way of identifying these temptations is sex, stuff, and self. Satan will throw out any one of these or a combination of them to trip up the spiritual leader and inflict damage on the leader and the people who follow him.

Satan's third strategy is *accusation*. In Revelation 12:10 we catch a glimpse into Satan's spiritual warfare plans. Here we see Satan revealed as "the accuser of our brothers . . . who accuses them day and night before our God." Satan goes to war against the Christian leader by unleashing a barrage of flaming accusations designed to defeat the leader or beat him down into quiet submission. Often these attacks center on the leader's lack of spiritual fitness, effectiveness, faith, or any other Christlike virtue. At the heart of this type of temptation is an attack on the pastor's identity in Christ. Leaders who know how to win this battle understand that Christians are not called to fight but to stand firm in their new identity in Christ with every piece of spiritual armor in place (see Ephesians 6:13–17). The devil's accusations are countered by the truth of who we are in Christ.

Think It Over: The Cost of Spiritual Warfare and Internal Battles

1. Which of the three schemes of the devil do you find most troubling?
2. Where is Satan's most regular point of attack toward you?
3. What are you doing to stay spiritually strong?

The Blessing of Deep Relationships

Despite the difficulties associated with pastoral ministry, a pastor finds many blessings and advantages to being a spiritual leader. One of those is the opportunity to develop deep relationships with various people.

A good leader will win the admiration and respect of many people and have an opportunity to grow deep relationships with some who will become lifelong friends. Look at the life of Jesus and we see the friendships that He built with Peter, James, and John, who made up the inner circle of His disciples. Whenever Jesus was in Jerusalem, He very likely stayed at the household of Lazarus, Mary, and Martha in nearby Bethany (see John 12:1–3). Paul's relationship with Timothy, Titus, Philemon, Tychicus,

Barnabas, Silas, Prisca and Aquila, and many others is testimony that Paul had Christian friends in many locations and at considerable depth.

Leaders need trusted friends who can speak into their lives when necessary and stand for them when needed. The portrait of a lone-wolf pastor who should not be allowed to make friends with anyone in the church is a tragic and dangerous one. The fear of showing favoritism should not rule out developing friendships. I have been blessed with faithful friends over the years who continue to be close and personal confidants long after I have moved from the ministry in which I met them. Even when my pastoral calling has taken me to serve in other countries, my friends and I have remained connected. Close friendships and deep caring relationships with individuals and married couples have been a blessing to my wife and me throughout our years in ministry.

Think It Over: The Blessing of Deep Relationships

1. Which people in your life strengthen your heart and give you joy?
2. What are you doing to deepen your relationships with these people?
3. What satisfies you the most about your friends?

The Blessing of a Life of Eternal Impact

Investing in people's lives for the cause of Christ lifts the ministry of a pastor to that of highest significance. At the top of the list of significant eternal impact is leading the unsaved to Christ. Over the years I have been privileged to personally lead neighbors, family members, airplane seatmates, fishing trip companions, counselees, the sick and the dying to faith in Jesus Christ.

Recently I hired an information technician to set up my computer. In the months before hiring him, my wife and I had built a relationship with this man and his wife. After he finished the job, he and I started talking about life, and eventually our conversation got around to the subject of Jesus. Within a half hour the young man was praying to receive Christ. That's significant!

A pastor's life is enriched when believers in his congregation experience exceptional spiritual growth. Early in Cornerstone's history I befriended a young man who owned a medical clinic. When he was asked to be a church leader, he worried that he could not fulfill this role. He confided in me that he felt unqualified because he had never prayed in public. Over the years, however, he has grown to the point at which he not only loves to pray in public but it's hard to stop him!

Another professional man who had never been in Christian leadership, along with his wife and seven other couples, stepped up to help plant Cornerstone Church. Within a few years Cornerstone was a strong and healthy church. With the lessons of faith and God's leading that this man and wife learned during our church startup, the two of them helped found another parachurch ministry that now ministers to hundreds each week.

Still another Christian businessman seemed so distant from serving the Lord that some people wondered if he was even saved. With some pastoral encouragement and spiritual growth, this man went on to become a leading missions advocate who today helps guide the evangelization of South Sudan.

The life of a leader has amazing potential to impact others who will impact the world. That's significant!

Think It Over: The Blessing of a Life of Eternal Impact

1. What or who comes to mind when you think of investing in others for eternal impact?
2. What makes these things or people so significant to you?
3. Who is the last person you led to Christ? Have you contacted that person recently to tell him how significant he is to you?

The Blessing of a Front-Row Seat to the Miraculous

The Bible tells of a woman who pushed her way through the crowd to Jesus because she had a serious medical problem:

> She came up behind him and touched the fringe of his garment, and immediately her discharge of blood ceased. And Jesus said, "Who was it that touched me?" When all denied it, Peter said, "Master, the crowds surround you and are pressing in on you!" But Jesus

> said, "Someone touched me, for I perceive that power has gone out from me." And when the woman saw that she was not hidden, she came trembling, and falling down before him declared in the presence of all the people why she had touched him, and how she had been immediately healed. And he said to her, "Daughter, your faith has made you well; go in peace." (Luke 8:44–48)

Why did this woman have to push her way through the crowd toward Jesus to touch Him? Because the crowds were all around Jesus, wanting to see what miracle He would do next.

One of the great privileges of Christian leadership is being in the front row of what God is doing. Pastors witness more miracles in a year than most believers see in a lifetime. Miraculous healings, deliverances, financial provision, restored marriages, dramatic protection from harm, needed guidance, employment, and much more.

In 2013 I was leading a tour in Israel, and a young Brazilian couple was part of the group. They had been married for seven years and had tried every avenue to overcome infertility. This nagging problem had caused great heartache in their marriage. My tour had scheduled in it a baptism in the Jordan River, and this young couple decided to follow Christ's command to be baptized. They both gave tearful testimonies of their faith in Jesus and then were baptized. As they came up out of the water, the Lord gave me a prophetic word for them, and I told them, "Next year at this time you will be pregnant with a child." Everyone heard me say this.

The couple looked surprised but pleased at the statement. The next year God miraculously gave them a beautiful baby girl! Being in the front row of the miraculous is a thrill and a blessing that God allows leaders to witness.

Think It Over: The Blessing of a Front-Row Seat to the Miraculous

1. What do you believe about God doing miracles today?
2. Recount some miracles you have witnessed.
3. To whom are miracles meant to point?

The Blessing of Giving and Receiving

God the Holy Spirit has placed everyone in body with spiritual gifts as He wills. One of the gifts of the Spirit is giving. Another blessing that leaders are privileged to experience is seeing God work through generous givers to accomplish His will. Through the years I have seen the Lord open the windows of heaven and pour out blessings that were hard to contain. Sometimes those financial blessings were directed to the ministry and other times they were given to bless my family and me.

For nineteen years I pastored in western Canada, where it rained for much of the year. Having grown up in sunny California, the change to a dark and rainy winter environment was hard for me. God knew how difficult it was for us, so He generously supplied a vacation for my family and me to sunny Hawaii in the middle of the winter one year. God used two men who didn't even know each other at the time to make it happen. We will never forget the orchestration of God's generosity through these two bighearted Christian friends.

Watch for God's generosity in many ways; babysitting, dental care, medical care, use of cabins, dinners, and so much more. The generosity of God's people is amazing and a huge blessing to leaders.

Think It Over: The Blessing of Giving and Receiving

1. Name some ways in which God has blessed you through the generosity of others.
2. How can you respond to this generosity with a grateful heart?
3. In what ways are you generous toward others?

The Blessing of God's Serendipities

Leadership puts pastors in places where they meet the most exceptional people in the most unexpected places. I could never have planned to become the close friend of a Chinese believer from Hong Kong who was an international businessman. God seated my wife and me at a convention right behind this man and his wife, and in a matter of only a few minutes, we established a friendship.

Over the next few years God deepened our friendship. Years later, when this man was asked to be the Queen of England's representative in British Columbia, Canada, he and his wife sought my advice as to the decision he should make. After we talked it over and prayed together, he went on to accept the honorable position. Who could have known that this man would become the first Asian man to represent the Queen of England? It was God's serendipity!

Think It Over: The Blessing of God's Serendipities

1. What are some unexpected gifts that God has given to you?
2. Have you shared God's goodness with anyone by giving them an unexpected gift of your time?

The Blessing of Personal Growth and Faith Stretching

By far the best blessing of being a pastoral leader is experiencing the personal growth that leadership affords. God develops His servants through the ups and downs of life.

The life of faith is not natural but supernatural. God uses pastors who are ready to step out and trust Him for what they cannot see. The constant thread that runs through the stories of all the men and women of God in the Bible is their faith. Faith is both the daily bread and the crown jewel of the Christian life. Without faith we cannot please God. Like bread, faith is the bare necessity leaders need to survive spiritually. Like the crown jewel, faith is the most precious gift that we can give to God.

Think It Over: The Blessing of Personal Growth and Faith Stretching

1. Name three ways in which you have grown by being a pastor.
2. How has being a pastor stretched your faith?
3. What has been your biggest faith moment to date?

CONCLUSION:
The Costs and Blessings of Being a Pastoral Leader

When we get to heaven and look back on our lives on this earth, we will not be impressed with our great achievements or the benefits we enjoyed; what will matter most about this life and the ministry we carried out on Earth will the times when life seemed difficult and the way was dark but we chose to trust God. From heaven's vantage point the days we had nothing but trusted God for everything will be life's finest moments.

Pastoring the flock of God is full of just such times. The call to shepherd God's people contains myriad challenges and difficulties that can make us tired, disillusioned, or afraid, and we must choose again and again to answer the call of God and stand firm in carrying out our ministry in the strength of the Lord.

Timothy faced great pressure when left on his own to exercise leadership over the body of Christ in Ephesus. The apostle Paul, knowing that he was soon to finish his own race and aware of his young disciple's fears amid the very real opposition that surrounded him, wrote to encourage him:

> I am reminded of your sincere faith, a faith that dwelt first in your grandmother Lois and your mother Eunice and now, I am sure, dwells in you as well. For this reason I remind you to fan into flame the gift of God, which is in you through the laying on of my hands, for God gave us a spirit not of fear but of power and love and self-control. (2 Timothy 1:5–7)

Have the costs of ministry ever threatened to overwhelm you? Have you been tempted to give way to pressure or fear or weariness? Maybe you are uncertain of your call; perhaps you have faced battles in your personal life; maybe you feel unqualified for the job of preaching or teaching or counseling. Or perhaps the increasing pressure from the world as we draw closer to the Lord's return have made you fearful. Take heart. Not only Timothy but also Moses and Joseph and David and Peter and Paul needed strengthening at times. Paul, knowing the great reward of finishing well as he faced the end of his earthly life and ministry, wrote firmly to his beloved son in the faith, "Continue in what you have learned and have firmly believed, knowing from whom you learned it. . . . I charge you in the presence of God and of Christ Jesus, who is to judge the living and the dead, and by his appearing and his kingdom: preach the word" (2 Timothy 3:14; 4:1–2).

The rewards of pastoral ministry will far outweigh its hardships. One day those pastors and leaders who have served the Lord faithfully will receive the ultimate blessing: "the crown of righteousness, which the Lord, the righteous judge, will award to . . . all who have loved his appearing" (2 Timothy 4:8). What a day that will be! "Therefore, my beloved brothers, be steadfast, immovable, always abounding in the work of the Lord, knowing that in the Lord your labor is not in vain" (1 Corinthians 15:58).

Until that day comes, may God give those who serve Him in the high calling of pastoral ministry many days of faithful and fruitful service. Soon the great Shepherd will come again, and the labor of shepherding His flock will end. On that day may His servants hear, "Well done, good and faithful servant. You have been faithful over a little; I will set you over much. Enter into the joy of your master" (Matthew 25:23). Then the shadow of this life will give way to heaven's glory forevermore.

APPENDIX 1

Things I Learned During a Time of Testing

During a time of personal crisis, when my call was tested, I learned a number of insights about myself, about people, and about God. Perhaps they will be of help to other pastors:

- "Listen" to what people *do*, not merely what they *say*.
- Pursue the truth in confusing situations to gain clarity and closure.
- Don't procrastinate when facing a difficult problem; deal with problems quickly and thoroughly.
- Don't let divisive people ruin the unity of the church.
- Avoid the danger of wanting to fit in rather than being who God made you to be. Courageously stand up for the person God made you to be.
- Keep trusted friends close at all times—you cannot predict when you will need their support or when they will need yours.
- Do not proudly think that you can ignore conventional wisdom and still succeed. If you do, you will eventually pay the price of your foolishness.
- Not everyone will like you or be at peace with you, no matter how hard you try to be at peace with them.
- When you embark on a difficult leadership direction, make sure that you have adequate prayer support, a just cause, a clear plan, and plenty of faith and patience.
- Remember those who were there for you in times of pain. Adversity separates acquaintances from true friends.

- God uses pain to teach valuable lessons that cannot be learned otherwise. Pain is the indispensible ingredient for growth in noble character.
- When the sorrow is too great, God is still there. Sometimes you cannot pray or believe God for yourself; that's when others must pray and believe for you the same way Aaron and Hur held up Moses' hands in battle.
- A godly wife who endures the storm with her husband and affirms him is one of God's greatest gifts to a leader.
- God allows unexpected and unwanted time-outs so that you can address other priorities.
- Not every situation can be worked out this side of heaven, no matter how much effort you exert or desire you have.
- When devastating trials come, God still blesses you in many ways. Look for the smaller and more profound blessings.
- Take courage—the end of a trial signals a new beginning.
- God redeems the most impossible situations, but He usually takes time to do it.

APPENDIX 2

A Godly Leader Versus a Fleshly Leader

King David Godly Appearance Inside	King Saul Royal Appearance Outside
David was God's kind of king (see 2 Samuel 7:8–16).	Saul was man's kind of king (see 1 Samuel 10:23–24).
David was a man after God's own heart (see Acts 13:22).	Saul was a man after people's praise (see 1 Samuel 18:6–8).
David's kingship was eternal through Christ (see 2 Samuel 7:29).	Saul's kingship was rejected (see 1 Samuel 15:23).
David was kind and benevolent (see 2 Samuel 9:6–8).	Saul was cruel (see 1 Samuel 20:30–32; 22:11–29).
David was forgiving (see 1 Samuel 26).	Saul was unforgiving (see 1 Samuel 14:44; 18:9).
David was penitent (see 2 Samuel 12:13; 24:10).	When confronted, Saul lied (see 1 Samuel 15:10–31).
David was courageous (see 1 Samuel 17:24–54; 1 Chronicles 18).	Saul was fearful (see 1 Samuel 17:11; 31:4–7).
David was at peace with God (see Psalm 4:8; 37:11).	Saul was separated from God (see 1 Samuel 16:14).

APPENDIX 3

The Powerful Influence of Speech

No human being can tame the tongue. It is a restless evil, full of deadly poison. (James 3:8)

Death and life are in the power of the tongue, and those who love it will eat its fruits. (Proverbs 18:21)

Whoever keeps his mouth and his tongue keeps himself out of trouble. (Proverbs 21:23)

I tell you, on the day of judgment people will give account for every careless word they speak, for by your words you will be justified, and by your words you will be condemned. (Matthew 12:36–37)

There is one whose rash words are like sword thrusts, but the tongue of the wise brings healing. (Proverbs 12:18)

Let no corrupting talk come out of your mouths, but only such as is good for building up, as fits the occasion, that it may give grace to those who hear. (Ephesians 4:29)

If anyone thinks he is religious and does not bridle his tongue but deceives his heart, this person's religion is worthless. (James 1:26)

A gentle tongue is a tree of life, but perverseness in it breaks the spirit. (Proverbs 15:4)

There are six things that the Lord hates, seven that are an abomination to him: haughty eyes, a lying tongue, and hands that shed innocent blood, a heart that devises wicked plans, feet that make haste to run to evil, a false witness who breathes out lies, and one who sows discord among brothers. (Proverbs 6:16–19)

I will guard my ways, that I may not sin with my tongue; I will guard my mouth with a muzzle, so long as the wicked are in my presence. (Psalm 39:1)

Everyone who is angry with his brother will be liable to judgment; whoever insults his brother will be liable to the council; and whoever says, "You fool!" will be liable to the hell of fire. (Matthew 5:22)

A false witness will not go unpunished, and he who breathes out lies will not escape. (Proverbs 19:5)

Whoever desires to love life and see good days, let him keep his tongue from evil and his lips from speaking deceit. (1 Peter 3:10)

Not many of you should become teachers, my brothers, for you know that we who teach will be judged with greater strictness. For we all stumble in many ways. And if anyone does not stumble in what he says, he is a perfect man, able also to bridle his whole body. If we put bits into the mouths of horses so that they obey us, we guide their whole bodies as well. Look at the ships also: though they are so large and are driven by strong winds, they are guided by a very small rudder wherever the will of the pilot directs. So also the tongue is a small member, yet it boasts of great things. How great a forest is set ablaze by such a small fire! (James 3:1–5)

Put away all malice and all deceit and hypocrisy and envy and all slander. (1 Peter 2:1)

The good person out of the good treasure of his heart produces good, and the evil person out of his evil treasure produces evil, for out of the abundance of the heart his mouth speaks. (Luke 6:45)

A man who bears false witness against his neighbor is like a war club, or a sword, or a sharp arrow. (Proverbs 25:18)

You have heard that it was said to those of old, "You shall not swear falsely, but shall perform to the Lord what you have sworn." But I say to you, Do not take an oath at all, either by heaven, for it is the throne of God, or by the earth, for it is his footstool, or by Jerusalem, for it is the city of the great King. And do not take an oath by your head, for you cannot make one hair white or black. Let what you say be simply "Yes" or "No"; anything more than this comes from evil. (Matthew 5:33–37)

If we confess our sins, he is faithful and just to forgive us our sins and to cleanse us from all unrighteousness. (1 John 1:9)

May the Lord cut off all flattering lips, the tongue that makes great boasts, those who say, "With our tongue we will prevail, our lips are with us; who is master over us?" (Psalm 12:3–4)

My son, be attentive to my wisdom; incline your ear to my understanding, that you may keep discretion, and your lips may guard knowledge. (Proverbs 5:1–2)

With patience a ruler may be persuaded, and a soft tongue will break a bone. (Proverbs 25:15)

If we say we have no sin, we deceive ourselves, and the truth is not in us. If we confess our sins, he is faithful and just to forgive us our sins and to cleanse us from all unrighteousness. If we say we have not sinned, we make him a liar, and his word is not in us. (1 John 1:8–10)

From the same mouth come blessing and cursing. My brothers, these things ought not to be so. (James 3:10)

A word fitly spoken is like apples of gold in a setting of silver. (Proverbs 25:11)

The Lord God has given me the tongue of those who are taught, that I may know how to sustain with a word him who is weary. Morning by morning he awakens; he awakens my ear to hear as those who are taught. (Isaiah 50:4)

When words are many, transgression is not lacking, but whoever restrains his lips is prudent. (Proverbs 10:19)

Let there be no filthiness nor foolish talk nor crude joking, which are out of place, but instead let there be thanksgiving. (Ephesians 5:4)

The tongue is a small member, yet it boasts of great things. How great a forest is set ablaze by such a small fire! (James 3:5)

APPENDIX 4

Divisions of Theology

Bibliology—doctrine of the Bible

- Preservation
- Inspiration
- Authority
- Inerrancy

Theology proper—doctrine of God

- The existence of God
- The attributes of God
- The Trinity
- Creation
- Divine providence

Anthropology—doctrine of man

- Created in God's image
- The fall into sin
- Death

Christology—doctrine of Christ

- Messianic prophecies
- Virgin birth
- Sinless life
- Miracles
- Teaching

- Death
- Resurrection

Soteriology—doctrine of salvation

- Atonement
- Redemption
- Regeneration
- Saving faith
- Security of the believer

Pneumatology—doctrine of the Holy Spirit

- Pentecost
- Power to witness
- Gifts
- Sealing
- Power to live

Ecclesiology—doctrine of the church

- Body of Christ
- Mission
- Ordinances
- Governance

Eschatology—doctrine of end times

- Promises of Christ's coming
- Rapture of the church
- Great tribulation
- Christ's second coming
- Christ's millennial reign
- Last judgment
- New heaven and earth

NOTES

Preface

1. Daniel Meyer, *Witness Essentials: Evangelism that Makes Disciples* (Downers Grove, IL: InterVarsity Press, 2012), 32–33.

Chapter 1: The Pastoral Leader and the Call to Ministry

1. Mark Tooley, "The Imploding and Very Liberal United Church of Canada," *Juicy Ecumenism*, August 18, 2012, https://juicyecumenism.com/2012/08/18/the-imploding-and-very-liberal-united-church-of-canada/ (accessed May 4, 2016).
2. Eusebius Pamphilius, *Church History*, Book III (Grand Rapids: Eerdmans, 2005), 4:6, http://www.ccel.org/ccel/schaff/npnf201.iii.viii.iv.html (accessed May 4, 2016).

Chapter 3: The Pastoral Leader's Personal Life

1. Jerry Rueb, *Design: Discover, Develop and Serve* (Long Beach, CA: Jerry Rueb, 2010).

Chapter 4: The Pastoral Leader as an Inspiring Trailblazer

1. Andrew Sobel, "Peter Drucker's Five Magic Questions," *Building Relationships for Life*, http://andrewsobel.com/peter-druckers-five-magic-questions/ (accessed May 4, 2016).

Chapter 6: The Pastoral Leader and Preaching

1. E. M. Bounds, *Power Through Prayer* (Incense House, 2013), 4.
2. John Pollock, *The Billy Graham Story* (Grand Rapids: Zondervan, 2003), 192.

Chapter 10: The Pastoral Leader and Church Organization

1. Ten insights on church growth and illustration, "Lifecycle of a Ministry: Organization or Institution?" adapted from George G. Hunter III (lecture, Biola University, La Mirada, CA, 2012) and *The Recovery of a Contagious Methodist Movement* (Nashville: Abingdon, 2011), 30–32.

RESOURCES BY

JERRY RUEB

Books and Booklets

Did Jesus Really Rise from the Dead?

For Those Who Ask

For Those Who Ask Workbook

Me or We . . . the Decision to Stay Single or Get Married

New Dimension Living

The Times of Your Life (coming soon)

Cornerstone Church Curriculum

Biblical Principles for Resolving Conflicts

Design: Six Milestones on the Journey of Discovering God's Unique Design for You

Friendship Evangelism

Team-Based Ministry with DVD Lay Counselor Training

DVD

Glimpses of Glory from the Shadow of Death

Sermons

www.cclb.org/watch-live---on-demand.html

Cornerstone Church Website

www.cclb.org

Some of the above resources as well as many other helpful materials can be found on the Cornerstone Church website at www.cclb.org/resources.